MEDITERRANEAN DIET

for Beginners:

❖❖❖❖❖

Easy and Healthy Recipes for Weight Loss & a 28-Day Meal Plan Program

D1569729

Madison Eaton

Table of Contents

Introduction to The Mediterranean Diet 6

    Principles of The Mediterranean Diet 6

    The Mediterranean Diet's Benefits 8

    Diet Meal Plan 8

    Diet Tips 9

Breakfast 10

    Mediterranean Omelette 11

    Egg White Breakfast Sandwich 12

    Egg Muffins with Veggies and Feta 13

    Honey Almond Ricotta Spread with Fruits 14

    Poached Eggs Caprese 15

    Mediterranean Breakfast Salad 16

    Eggs Florentine 17

    Breakfast Quinoa 18

    Mediterranean Breakfast Buns 19

    Breakfast Tostadas 20

    Mediterranean Frittata 21

    Baked Eggs and Zoodles 22

    Banana Mocha Oats 23

    Hummus and Veggies Bowl 24

    Avocado and Apple Smoothie 25

    Berry Chia Overnight Oats 26

    Savory Steel Cut Oatmeal 27

    Eggs Baked in Tomatoes 28

Lunch 29

    Eggplant Pizza 30

    Kale Chickpeas Grain Bowl 31

    Lamb and Beet Meatballs 32

    Shrimp and Leek Spaghetti 33

Pasta Salad with Tomatoes and Eggplant 34

Balela Salad 35

Fattoush Salad 36

Tuna Salad with Dijon Mustard Vinaigrette 37

White Bean Soup 38

Lentil Soup 39

Vegetable Soup 40

Mediterranean Chicken Soup 41

Lemony Escarole Soup 42

Dinner

Dinner 43

Couscous with Tuna and Pepperoncini 44

Mediterranean Cod 45

Shrimp with Pineapple Rice 46

Lemon Chicken with Asparagus 47

Cilantro Lime Chicken 48

Shrimp And Leek Spaghetti 49

Panko Salmon With Snap Peas 50

Gnocchi With Spinach And Pepper Sauce 51

Chicken And Bulgur Salad With Peaches 52

Greek Turkey Burgers 53

Orange-Balsamic Lamb Chops 54

Seared Mediterranean Tuna Steaks 55

Greek-Style Scampi 56

Couscous With Artichokes,Feta And Sun-Dried Tomatoes 57

Pasta With Sun-Dried Tomato Pesto And Feta Cheese 58

Mussels In Spicy Tomato Sauce 59

Easy Stuffed Peppers 60

Mediterranean Vegetables With Lamb 61

Mediterranean Chicken Tray Bake 62

Desserts

Desserts 63

Tiramisu 64

Italian Apple Olive Oil Cake 65

Greek Cheesecake with Yogurt 66

Greek Yogurt and Honey Walnuts... 67

Chocolate Brownies.. 68

Peach Nectarine Mango Crumble 69

Cherry Clafoutis.. 70

Blood Orange Olive Oil Cake.. 71

Gluten-Free Lemon Cake... 72

Yogurt and Honey Olive Oil Cake.. 73

Snacks.. 74

Greek Yogurt Spinach Artichoke Dip 75

Fig Smoothie With Cinnamon... 76

Smoked Salmon,Avocado And Cucumber Bites 77

Baked Root Vegetable Chips With Buttermilk-Parsley Dipping Sauce.......... 78

Spicy Red Lentil Dip 79

Cucumber Hummus Sandwiches 80

Blackberries Caprese Skewers 81

Tomato-Basil Skewers 82

Fig and Ricotta Toast... 83

Date Wraps.. 84

Week 1.. 85

Shopping List 85

Day 1 87

Day 2 87

Day 3 87

Day 4 87

Day 5 87

Day 6 87

Day 7 87

Week 2.. 88

Shopping List 88

Day 1 90

Day 2 90

Day 3 90

Day 4 90

Day 5 90

Day 6 90

Day 7 90

Week 3 91

Shopping List 91

Day 1 93

Day 2 93

Day 3 93

Day 4 93

Day 5 93

Day 6 93

Day 7 93

Week 4 94

Shopping List 94

Day 1 96

Day 2 96

Day 3 96

Day 4 96

Day 5 96

Day 6 96

Day 7 96

Introduction to The Mediterranean Diet

Principles of The Mediterranean Diet

The Mediterranean diet is a rather simple diet based on the national cuisine of different Mediterranean countries. It's a great example of a balanced diet, in which vegetable proteins are the main source of nutrients. The scientists paid close attention to this diet after they studied health habits of people from Greece and Italy. In their research, scientists tracked eating habits of about 3,000 men and women from Greece aged 18 to 89 who didn't suffer from cardiovascular diseases. The research showed that the more people adhered to the Mediterranean diet, they lowered their levels of inflammation that can cause heart disease.

Studies have shown that a low-fat diet rich in fruits and vegetables can prevent heart disease. The Mediterranean diet is based on fruits, vegetables, fish, and olive oil, so it has very little meat.

The main principles of the Mediterranean diet involve:
- Everyday consumption of bread and cereals, pasta, corn, couscous, barley, etc.
- Everyday consumption of fruits and vegetables
- Everyday consumption of beans, nuts, olive oil, and/or other healthy oils
- 3-5 times a week consumption of dairy products, seafood, eggs, and poultry
- Once a week consumption of sweets and red meat
- Everyday consumption of at least 2 l of water
- 1-2 glasses of red wine a day is also acceptable

Carbohydrates: pasta and porridge
Whole pasta, bread, rice, and cereals are good for health and you need them every day. However, you must to reduce the consumption of refined carbohydrates such as whole milk and cottage cheese will have to be limited.

Vegetables and Fruits
You can eat any vegetables: potatoes, all varieties of cabbage, peppers, tomatoes, eggplant, leeks, carrots, zucchini, olives, and olives. Nutritionists claim that olives (both green and black) are rich in vitamins A, C, E and contain healthy vegetable

fats, sugar, proteins, and pectins. Regular daily intake of vegetables and fruits should be about 1 kg.

The main vegetables in Mediterranean cuisine are onions and tomatoes, both raw and cooked. Besides giving a special zest for food, onions also have specific nutritional value. They don't contain cholesterol and fat. At the same time, they're rich in phytochemicals, as well as antimicrobial properties. Onions also contain flavonoids, which have strong antioxidant effect. Thus, onions can help prevent cardiovascular disease, as they're involved in the regulation of sugar, cholesterol, and triglycerides.

Tomatoes are mainly used in preparation of hot dishes as they contain antioxidant lycopene contained which is better absorbed by the body when hot. Lycopene is one of the most powerful antioxidants due to its ability to neutralize the harmful free oxygen radicals that cause mutations in DNA cells. This, for example, reduces the risk of prostate cancer. At the same time, the consumption of tomatoes improves brain function as they're rich in potassium, which regulates blood pressure.

Proteins: meat, fish, eggs
In a Mediterranean diet, grass-fed and lean meat is the basis of healthy eating plan. You need to eat fresh fish, seafood (lobster, squid, mussels and scallops) and lean meat regularly (at least 5 times a week). It's also important to add vegetable oils to the plan. Menu also should include eggs (no more than 2-4 eggs per week). Dairy products should also be included - natural yogurts and a piece of cheese or a glass of low-fat kefir or milk per day.

Chicken meat also plays a key role in the diet plan as it's rich in nutritious and easily digestible proteins, as well as B vitamins, which strengthen the nervous system.

Olive oil
Another prime ingredient of the Mediterranean diet plan is olive oil. Numerous studies insist that it's rich in monounsaturated fatty acids and antioxidants; it also prevents coronary heart disease and lowers bad cholesterol levels.

The Mediterranean Diet's Benefits

This diet has many benefits you'll feel the different from the first few weeks after you begin following it. The main advantages are:

- It's easier than many other popular diets. You don't need to change your lifestyle completely: all you need is just to reconsider what products you use for cooking and to modify your daily meal plan.
- The diet may reduce the risk of serious illnesses.
- Improves your skin, thus it helps to look younger. Increases longevity.
- Reducing the risk of Alzheimer's and Parkinson's disease.
- Helps to reduce the consumption of processed products.
- The diet is a balanced combination of natural products, moderate consumption of red meat and wine.
- Suitable for vegetarians, since it offers a variety of dishes.

Diet Meal Plan

Breakfast should always be a main component in your daily meal plan. It should contain carbohydrates (cereals) and dinner should infuse protein and vegetables. Thus, you'll have energy for the whole day and you won't gain weight because you eat carbs in the first half of the day. Honey and/or jam are usually served along with bread. Pasta, rice, and vegetables are usually served for lunch.

The key to success to Mediterranean diet is dividing food into small portions. You shouldn't count on fast and radical weight loss but rather on gradual and healthy weight loss with this diet.

The main point is to reduce the portion size and daily food intake, gradually moving to a healthier diet without high-calorie and carbohydrate-rich foods. According to different researches, the Mediterranean diet helps to improve the body shape as well as your skin, improve eyesight, lower blood cholesterol, and keep the cardiovascular system in perfect condition. In addition, it's much easier than other popular diets.

Diet Tips

The best tips that you can follow to succeed in Mediterranean diet are:

1. Plan your meal. All the dishes in Mediterranean diet are usually very easy to cook, but most of them have to be consumed when fresh. You can still refrigerate the cooked pasta, but it won't taste the same the next day. Thus, plan your meal ahead; you can cook the same dish the next day if you want, since it won't take you long.
2. Eat more fish. Fish is rich in healthy nutrients and is great for your body. Eat fish more often than you eat meat.
3. Use olive oil, less butter.
4. Make the salad dressings yourself. There are so many recipes for salad dressings, so you can try them all.
5. Add a glass of wine to your meal plan. Remember about the limit though, and aim for one glass for women and two glasses for men.

Following the Mediterranean diet can reduce risk of heart disease, obesity, type II diabetes, and other diseases. In this cookbook you'll find easy and delicious Mediterranean recipes for Breakfast, Lunch, Dinner, and Desserts that you can cook in no time and stay healthy.

This cookbook will be useful both for beginners and for those who already follows this diet. So choose the recipes you like the most, go shopping, and start enjoying healthy Mediterranean dishes

Breakfast

Mediterranean Omelette

Prep time: 10 minutes   **Servings:** 1

Ingredients

- 1/2 tomato, diced
- 1 teaspoon oil or butter
- 1 tablespoon feta, crumbled
- 2 eggs
- 1 artichoke heart, quartered
- 2 tablespoons Kalamata olives, sliced
- 1 tablespoon milk or cream
- 1 tablespoon Romesco sauce
- Salt and pepper, to taste

Instructions

1. Beat eggs with salt and pepper in a bowl.
2. Heat oil in a skillet, add eggs. Cover the bottom of the pan evenly. Cook until the eggs begin to set, and then add tomatoes, along with artichokes, olives, and feta to one half of the omelette. Fold it in half.
3. Let the eggs cook until set for about 1 minute. Remove from the heat and top with Romesco sauce. Serve and enjoy!

Nutritional info (per serving): 303 calories; 17.7g fat; 21.9 g total carbs; 18.2 g protein

Egg White Breakfast Sandwich

Prep time: 20 minutes

Servings: 3-4

Ingredients

- 1/2 cup roasted tomatoes
- 1 teaspoon butter
- 1–2 slices Muenster cheese
- 1/4 cup egg whites
- 1 tablespoon pesto
- Salt, pepper, to taste
- 1 whole grain seeded ciabatta roll
- 1 teaspoon fresh herbs such as basil, parsley, and rosemary, chopped

For Roasted Tomatoes:
- 1 tablespoon extra-virgin olive oil
- 10 oz. grape tomatoes, halved
- Salt, pepper, to taste

Instructions

1. To a nonstick skillet, add a teaspoon of butter and melt it over medium heat; then add egg whites and sprinkle with pepper, salt and fresh herbs. Cook until the eggs are completely cooked through, for about 3-4 minutes, flipping once.
2. In the meantime, start toasting the ciabatta bread in your toaster. Once toasted, spread the pesto on both halves.
3. Top the bottom half of sandwich roll with egg followed by cheese. Now add 1/2 cup roasted tomatoes and top with another half of the roll.
4. For roasted tomatoes: spread the tomatoes on a baking sheet and drizzle with olive oil; toss well until coated. Season with pepper and salt to taste. Roast in a preheated oven at 400 F, for 20 minutes.

Nutritional info (per serving): 458 calories; 24 g fat; 51 g total carbs; 21 g protein

Egg Muffins with Veggies and Feta

Prep time: 30 minutes　　　　**Servings:** 12

Ingredients

- 8 eggs
- 2 cups baby spinach, chopped
- 1 cup feta cheese, crumbled
- 1 tablespoon fresh oregano, chopped
- 1/2 cup onion, chopped
- 1 cup tomatoes, cherry, or grape tomatoes, chopped or sliced
- 1 cup quinoa, cooked
- 1/2 cup Kalamata olives, chopped, pitted
- 1/4 teaspoon salt
- 2 teaspoons sunflower oil

Instructions

1. Preheat the oven to 350F. Grease a 12 muffin tin. Set aside.
2. Add oil to a skillet placed over medium heat. Add onions to the skillet and sauté for 2 minutes, then add tomatoes. Continue sautéing for additional 1 minute, and then add spinach. Sauté for about 1 minute until the spinach have wilted. Turn the heat off, stir in oregano along with olives. Set aside.
3. To a blender or a mixing bowl, add the eggs and process thoroughly until well combined. If using a blender, pour the eggs into a mixing bowl and add in quinoa along with feta cheese, salt, and the veggie mixture. Stir until well combined.
4. When done, pour the mixture into the prepared muffins or silicone cups as. Bake in the preheated oven for about 30 minutes.
5. Leave to cool for 5 minutes and serve. Enjoy!

Nutritional info (per serving): 114 calories; 7g fat; 6 g total carbs; 7 g protein

Honey Almond Ricotta Spread with Fruits

Prep time: 15 minutes

Servings: 4-6

Ingredients

For Ricotta Spread:
- 1/4 teaspoon almond extract
- 1 orange, zested
- 1 cup whole milk ricotta
- 1 teaspoons honey
- 1/2 cup almonds, sliced

For Serving:
- Peaches, sliced
- Extra honey, for drizzling
- Hearty whole grain toast, English muffin, or bagel
- Extra sliced almonds

Instructions

1. Mix 1/4 teaspoon almond extract, 1/2 cup almonds and 1 cup whole milk ricotta in a bowl; stir well.
2. Transfer to a serving platter; sprinkle with sliced almonds and drizzle with honey.
3. Toast the bread and top with the ricotta spread.
4. Top the ricotta spread with sliced peaches, followed by sliced almonds and honey.

Nutritional info (per serving): 132 calories; 8.2 g fat; 8 g total carbs; 7 g protein

Poached Eggs Caprese

Prep time: 20 minutes

Servings: 2

Ingredients

- 2 English muffin, halved
- 1 tablespoon distilled white vinegar
- 4 teaspoons pesto
- 2 teaspoons salt
- 1 tomato, thickly sliced
- 4 eggs
- 4 (1 oz.) slices mozzarella cheese
- Salt, to taste

Instructions

1. Pour water into a saucepan and bring to a light boil. Turn the heat down and then add 2 teaspoons of salt, along with 1 tablespoon distilled white vinegar; bring to a simmer.
2. In the meantime, top each muffin half with a slice of tomato, followed by slice of mozzarella cheese; toast for about 5 minutes until cheese softens.
3. Crack an egg into a small bowl and slip it gently into the simmering water. Repeat the same process with the remaining eggs.
4. Poach for about 2 1/2 to 3 minutes, until yolks have thickened and whites are firm.
5. Remove the eggs from water with a slotted spoon and transfer to a clean towel. Top each muffin with the poached egg and pesto. Season with salt. Serve.

Nutritional info (per serving): 546 calories; 30g fat; 30 g total carbs; 38 g protein

Mediterranean Breakfast Salad

Prep time: 10 minutes

Servings: 4

Ingredients

- 1 avocado
- 4 eggs, soft boiled
- 1 cup quinoa, cooked, cooled
- 10 cups arugula
- 1/2 cup mixed herbs, chopped
- 2 cups cherry tomatoes, halved
- 1 cup almonds, chopped
- 1/2 cucumber, seedless, chopped
- 1 lemon
- Sea salt and black pepper, to taste

Instructions

1. Peel the cooked eggs and cut in half.
2. Combine arugula with the tomatoes, quinoa, and cucumber in a bowl, and then drizzle with little olive oil. Season well with salt and pepper; then toss the ingredients.
3. When through, divide the salad among the serving plates, then top with the sliced avocado and halved egg. Sprinkle with almonds and herbs, and then season with additional salt and pepper and add a squeeze of lemon juice.
4. Finally, drizzle with olive oil and serve. Enjoy!

Nutritional info (per serving): 332 calories; 18.6 g fat; 30 g total carbs; 15 g protein

Eggs Florentine

Prep time: 10 minutes

Servings: 3

Ingredients

- 6 eggs, slightly beaten
- 2 tablespoons butter
- 1/2 package (10 oz.) fresh spinach
- 1/2 cup mushrooms, sliced
- 3 tablespoons cream cheese, cut into small pieces
- 2 garlic cloves, minced
- Salt and ground black pepper, to taste

Instructions

1. Melt the butter in a skillet over medium heat, cook the mushrooms and garlic as you stir for 1 minute until the garlic is fragrant.
2. Add the spinach to the mushroom mixture and cook for 2-3 minutes until the spinach has wilted.
3. Stir in the eggs and season with salt and pepper. Cook until the eggs begin to firm up without stirring, and then flip.
4. Top with cream cheese and cook for about 5 minutes until the cream cheese begins to soften. Serve and enjoy!

Nutritional info (per serving): 279 calories; 22.9g fat; 4.1 g total carbs; 15.7 g protein

Breakfast Quinoa

Prep time: 10 minutes

Servings: 4

Ingredients

- 2 cups milk
- 1/4 cup raw almonds, chopped
- 1 teaspoon vanilla extract
- 1 teaspoon ground cinnamon
- 2 dates, dried, pitted, chopped
- 1 cup quinoa
- 2 tablespoons honey
- 5 dried apricots, finely chopped
- 1 teaspoon sea salt

Instructions

1. Over medium heat, toast the almonds in a skillet for about 3-5 minutes until just golden and set aside.
2. Heat the cinnamon, along with the quinoa, in a saucepan over medium heat until warmed through, then add in milk and sea salt.
3. Stir the mixture and bring to a boil. Reduce the heat to low and close the lid. Cook for 15 minutes over low heat, and then stir in vanilla along with dates, honey, apricots, and around ½ of the almonds.
4. Top with the remaining almonds and serve. Enjoy!

Nutritional info (per serving): 327 calories; 7.9g fat; 53.9 g total carbs; 11.5 g protein

Mediterranean Breakfast Buns

Prep time: 20 minutes

Servings: 4-6

Ingredients

- 4-5 eggs, beaten
- 3 tablespoons butter
- 1 ½ cups sharp Cheddar cheese, shredded
- ½ cup fresh shiitake mushrooms, diced
- 11 oz. Pillsbury thin pizza crust, refrigerated
- 2 spinach and feta chicken sausages, smoked, chopped
- 1/8 teaspoon black pepper
- 1 cup fresh baby spinach, loosely packed, chopped
- 1/8 teaspoon kosher salt
- 6 fresh sage leaves

Instructions

1. Preheat the oven to 400F and line a cooking pan with parchment paper.
2. Melt 1 tablespoon of butter in a skillet over medium heat, then add mushrooms and sausage. Cook as you stir frequently until the sausage is heated through and the mushrooms are tender, for about 3-4 minutes; next, remove from the skillet and set aside on a plate.
3. Beat the eggs together with salt and pepper in a bowl using a whisk until well beaten.
4. Melt 1 tablespoon of butter in the same skillet over medium heat, then add the egg mixture. Cook as you stir frequently for about 2-3 minutes, and then add in ¾ cup of cheese. Remove from the heat and let cool for 10 minutes.
5. Sprinkle a cutting board lightly with flour, then unroll the pizza dough on the board. Shape the dough into a rectangle, then top with the remaining ¾ cup of cheese, sausage mixture and the eggs, then slightly press down, and sprinkle the chopped spinach over the eggs evenly.
6. Roll the dough into a wrap. Place the seam side down on the cutting board and cut into 6 equal slices. Place onto the baking mat. Bake until golden brown, for about 13-15 minutes.
7. In the meantime, melt the remaining 1 tablespoon of butter in another skillet over medium heat, add sage leaves. Cook as you stir frequently until crisp, for about 1-2 minutes. Remove the sage leaves to a paper towel and crumble them, reserve the butter.
8. When through, remove the buns from the oven and brush the sides with the reserved sage butter. Bake for additional 1 minute; sprinkle each bun with crumbled sage leaves. Serve warm and enjoy!

Nutritional info (per serving): 287 calories; 18.8 g fat; 16 g total carbs; 13 g protein

Breakfast Tostadas

Prep time: 5 minutes

Servings: 4

Ingredients

- ½ cup cucumber, seeded, chopped
- 4 tostadas
- ½ teaspoon garlic powder
- ½ cup red pepper hummus, roasted
- ½ cup skim milk
- 8 eggs, beaten
- ½ cup red pepper, diced
- ½ cup tomatoes, diced
- ½ cup green onions, chopped
- ½ teaspoon oregano
- ¼ cup feta, crumbled

Instructions

1. Add the red peppers to a non-stick skillet placed over medium heat and cook until softened, for about 2-3 minutes. Add in the eggs along with milk, oregano, garlic powder, and green onions and cook as you stir constantly for about 2 minutes.
2. When done, top each tostada with the egg mixture, hummus, cucumber, tomatoes, and feta. Serve immediately and enjoy!

Nutritional info (per serving): 320 calories; 21.5 g fat; 10 g total carbs; 21 g protein

Mediterranean Frittata

Prep time: 22 minutes   **Servings:** 4

Ingredients

- 1 tablespoon olive oil
- 6 eggs
- ½ cup basil leaves, fresh, torn
- 2 egg whites
- 1 cup Parmesan cheese
- 1 lb. asparagus, trimmed, cut into 1-inch pieces
- 1 leek, sliced
- Salt and pepper, to taste
- 8 oz. baby Bella mushrooms, sliced
- 1 cup goat cheese

Instructions

1. Preheat the oven to 400F.
2. Whisk eggs together with the egg whites in a bowl, and then stir in the Parmesan, along with the basil. Season with desired salt and pepper and set aside.
3. Heat the oil in a nonstick skillet placed over medium heat, and then add in the leeks. Cook as you stir occasionally until the leeks are starting to soften, about 3 minutes. Add the asparagus to the skillet, along with mushrooms, and cook as you stir occasionally until mushrooms and asparagus are soft and the mushrooms have released most of the moisture.
4. Pour the egg mixture into the skillet. Cook for about 2 minutes, then sprinkle with the goat cheese. Bake until the center is set, for about 10-12 minutes.
5. Loosen the edges with a spatula, then slide frittata onto the serving plate. Serve immediately and enjoy!

Nutritional info (per serving): 430 calories; 29g fat; 11 g total carbs; 34 g protein

Baked Eggs and Zoodles

Prep time: 15 minutes

Servings: 2

Ingredients

- 2 avocados, halved, thinly sliced
- 4 eggs
- 2 tablespoons olive oil, extra-virgin
- 3 zucchini, spiralized into noodles
- Salt and pepper, to taste
- Fresh basil, to garnish
- Red-pepper flakes, to garnish

Instructions

1. Preheat the oven to 350F and grease a baking sheet lightly with the cooking spray.
2. Toss the zucchini noodles in a bowl together with olive oil until combined. Season with salt and pepper, then divide into 4 portions evenly.
3. Transfer to the greased baking sheet and shape each into a nest.
4. Crack an egg gently into the center of each nest and bake in the preheated oven for about 9-11 minutes until the eggs are set.
5. Season with salt and pepper, then garnish with basil and the red pepper flakes.
6. Serve alongside avocado slices and enjoy!

Nutritional info (per serving): 633 calories; 53g fat; 27 g total carbs; 20 g protein

Banana Mocha Oats

Prep time: 15 minutes

Servings: 2

Ingredients

- 1 cup rolled oats
- 1 banana
- 1 ½ tablespoons chia seeds
- ¾ cup almond milk or any non-dairy milk of choice
- 2 tablespoons cocoa powder
- ½ cup strong coffee
- 1/8 teaspoon sea salt
- 2 dates, pitted, soaked in warm water for 1 hour, blended
- Fresh fruit, to serve

Instructions

1. Add the banana, coffee, cocoa powder, dates, salt, and almond milk to a blender and process until smooth.
2. Place the oats in an airtight container along with the chia seeds, then pour the liquid mixture over the oats and chia seeds. Stir everything together until well combined.
3. Cover the container and set to refrigerate overnight. Next, then stir the oats again in the morning. Add in a small splash of extra non-dairy milk and finally, top with the fresh fruits.
4. Serve and enjoy!

Nutritional info (per serving): 319 calories; 10 g fat; 68 g total carbs; 13 g protein

Hummus and Veggies Bowl

Prep time: 5 minutes   **Servings:** 4

Ingredients

- 1 ½ cups quinoa, cooked
- 1 tablespoon olive oil
- ½ cup hummus
- 3 cups Brussels sprouts, shredded
- 1 lb. asparagus, trimmed and chopped
- 1 avocado, peeled, pitted, sliced
- 3 cups kale leaves, shredded
- 4 eggs, cooked

For the Dressing:
- 1 garlic clove, minced
- 2 tablespoons olive oil
- 2 teaspoons Dijon mustard
- 2 tablespoons lemon juice
- Salt and black pepper, to taste

Instructions

1. Heat the oil in a cooking pan over medium heat, then add asparagus. Saute as you stir occasionally for about 4-5 minutes until the asparagus is tender. Remove from the heat. Set aside.
2. In the meantime, combine all the dressing ingredients in a bowl. Add the kale, and then massage the dressing into the kale, for about 2-3 minutes.
3. Add the Brussels sprouts to the mixing bowl, along with the quinoa, and cooked asparagus, toss well to combine.
4. Assemble the bowls. Add 1 spoonful of hummus to the side of each bowl, then divide the kale salad between the bowls evenly. Top with avocado, egg, and your preferred garnishes.
5. Serve immediately and enjoy!

Nutritional info (per serving): 650 calories; 34.2 g fat; 65 g total carbs; 26 g protein

Avocado and Apple Smoothie

Prep time: 5 minutes   **Servings:** 2

Ingredients

- 1 avocado
- 3 cups spinach
- 1 banana, frozen
- 1 teaspoon honey
- 1 apple, chopped
- 3 tablespoons chia seeds
- 2 cups coconut water

Instructions

1. Add the spinach, coconut water, and apple to a blender and process until smooth.
2. Add in the avocado, chia seeds, frozen banana, and honey and continue blending until creamy and smooth.
3. Pour into chilled glasses and serve immediately. Enjoy!

Nutritional info (per serving): 417 calories; 21g fat; 55 g total carbs; 25 g protein

Berry Chia Overnight Oats

Prep time: 5 minutes

Servings: 2

Ingredients

- 1 cup milk
- 1/2 cup rolled oats
- 1 cup berries of choice, frozen
- 1/8 teaspoon salt
- 1/4 cup chia seeds
- 1/8 teaspoon cinnamon
- Maple syrup, to taste
- Berries, for topping
- Yogurt, for topping

Instructions

1. Add oats, milk, seeds, salt, and cinnamon to a jar with a lid and refrigerate overnight.
2. Puree the berries in a blender, and then stir the oats together with the frozen berry puree.
3. Top with additional berries and yogurt, honey, nuts, or any desired toppings.
4. Serve and enjoy!

Nutritional info (per serving): 516 calories; 16.5 g fat; 78.1 g total carbs; 14.8 g protein

Savory Steel Cut Oatmeal

Prep time: 35 minutes

Servings: 4

Ingredients

- 1 cup steel-cut oats
- 3 cups water
- 1 tablespoon olive oil
- 1 cup milk
- ¼ teaspoon salt
- Toppings of your choice (grated cheese, sauteed veggies, etc.)

Instructions

1. Combine water and milk in a saucepan and then bring the mixture to a simmer over medium heat.
2. Meanwhile, melt the olive oil in a skillet placed over medium heat. Add in the oats and cook as you stir occasionally for about 2 minutes until fragrant and golden.
3. Stir the oats into the simmering water-milk mixture and reduce the heat to medium low. Allow to simmer gently as you stir occasionally until the mixture has become very thick, for about 20-25 minutes.
4. Stir in the salt and continue stirring the mixture for about 10 minutes. Remove from the heat.
5. Let it rest for 5 minutes. Season with more salt, pepper, and optional spices, and then stir in any mix-ins of your choice.

Nutritional info (per serving): 125 calories; 7g fat; 18 g total carbs; 6 g protein

Eggs Baked in Tomatoes

Prep time: 20 minutes

Servings: 4

Ingredients

- 8 tomatoes
- 8 eggs
- ¼ cup milk
- 2 tablespoons olive oil
- 4 tablespoons fresh herbs, chopped
- ¼ cup Parmesan cheese, grated
- Salt and black pepper, to taste

Instructions

1. Preheat the oven to 375F and grease an oven-safe skillet with olive oil.
2. Cut out the stems of tomatoes and scoop out all the flesh with a spoon. Reserve the flesh for salsa or tomato sauce.
3. Arrange the tomato shells in the greased skillet, then crack 1 egg into each tomato. Top each egg with a tablespoon of milk and a tablespoon of parmesan cheese, then season each egg with salt and pepper.
4. Bake for about 15-17 minutes. Let cool for 5 minutes, then garnish with fresh herbs and serve immediately. Enjoy!

Nutritional info (per serving): 288 calories; 19g fat; 12 g total carbs; 18 g protein

Lunch

Eggplant Pizza

Prep time: 25 minutes

Servings: 6

Ingredients

- 1 ½ cups mozzarella cheese, shredded
- 2 medium eggplants, trimmed and cut into ¾ inch thick slices
- 2 cups cherry tomatoes, halved
- ⅓ cup olive oil
- 1¼ cups marinara sauce, store-bought or homemade
- Salt and pepper, to taste
- ½ cup basil leaves, torn

Instructions

1. Preheat the oven to 400F and line a baking sheet with parchment paper.
2. Arrange the eggplant slices on the lined baking sheets. Brush the slices with olive oil on both sides, and then season with salt and pepper.
3. Roast in the preheated oven for about 10-12 minutes until almost tender.
4. Remove from the oven and spread 2 tablespoons of marinara sauce on top of each eggplant piece, then generously top with mozzarella. Arrange 3-5 cherry tomato pieces on top of each.
5. Place the pizzas back into the oven and roast for about 5-7 minutes. Serve the pizzas while still hot and garnish with the torn basil leaves. Enjoy!

Nutritional info (per serving): 257 calories; 20 g fat; 13 g total carbs; 8 g protein

Kale Chickpeas Grain Bowl

Prep time: 20 minutes   **Servings:** 4

Ingredients

- 2 tablespoons olive oil
- 1 cup water, boiling
- 1/2 avocado, peeled, pitted
- 1/2 cup bulgur, uncooked
- 1 garlic clove
- 1 tablespoon water
- 2 (15 oz. each) cans chickpeas, unsalted, rinsed, drained
- 1/2 teaspoon black pepper
- 1 1/2 tablespoons canola oil
- 3/4 teaspoon kosher salt, divided
- 2 cups carrots, chopped
- 1 tablespoon fresh lemon juice
- 4 cups lacinato kale, chopped
- 1/2 cup shallots, vertically sliced
- 1 tablespoon tahini
- 1/2 cup flat-leaf parsley leaves, chopped
- 1/4 teaspoon ground turmeric

Instructions

1. In a bowl, combine a cup of boiling water and bulgur. Next, let stand for 10 minutes. Drain well.
2. Pat dry the chickpeas with paper towels. Heat the canola oil in a skillet over high heat, then add chickpeas along with carrots. Cook for about 6 minutes as you stir occasionally until the chickpeas are nicely browned.
3. Add the kale and cover. Cook for about 2 minutes until the kale has wilted slightly and the carrots have become tender.
4. Add the chickpea mixture to the bulgur along with shallots, ½ teaspoon of salt, pepper, and parsley. Toss well.
5. Add the avocado, juice, tahini, olive oil, 1 tablespoon of water, turmeric, garlic, and the remaining ¼ teaspoon of salt to a food process and process until smooth.
6. Divide the bulgur mixture among the serving bowls and drizzle with avocado mixture evenly. Serve and enjoy!

Nutritional info (per serving): 520 calories; 20 g fat; 68 g total carbs; 18 g protein

Lamb and Beet Meatballs

Prep time: 20 minutes   **Servings:** 4

Ingredients

- 1 tablespoon olive oil
- 1 (8 oz.) package beets, cooked
- 6 oz. ground lamb
- 1/2 cup bulgur, uncooked
- 1 teaspoon ground cumin
- 1/2 cup cucumber, grated
- 1/2 cup sour cream, reduced-fat
- 2 tablespoons fresh mint, thinly sliced
- 2 tablespoons fresh lemon juice
- 1 oz. almond flour
- 4 cups mixed baby greens
- 3/4 teaspoon kosher salt
- 3/4 teaspoon freshly ground black pepper

Instructions

1. Preheat the oven to 425F.
2. Add the beets to a food processor and pulse until finely chopped, Then combine the chopped beets with bulgur, lamb, cumin, ½ teaspoon of salt, pepper, and almond flour in a bowl.
3. Divide the lamb mixture and shape it into 12 meatballs.
4. Heat the oil in a skillet over medium-high heat, then add into prepared meatballs. Cook until nicely browned on all sides, for about 4 minutes.
5. Transfer the browned meatballs to the preheated oven and bake until well cooked, about 8 minutes.
6. Combine the remaining ¼ teaspoon of salt together with cucumber, juice, mint, and sour cream in a bowl, then divide the greens among the serving plates.
7. Top the greens with the meatballs evenly and serve with the cucumber mixture. Enjoy!

Nutritional info (per serving): 338 calories; 21 g fat; 25 g total carbs; 14 g protein

Shrimp and Leek Spaghetti

Prep time: 20 minutes   **Servings:** 4

Ingredients

- 2 cups leek, chopped
- 8 oz. spaghetti, uncooked, whole-grain
- 1/4 cup heavy cream
- 1 lb. raw medium shrimp, peeled, deveined
- 2 teaspoons lemon zest
- 1 tablespoon garlic, chopped
- 1/2 teaspoon black pepper
- 2 cups baby sweet peas, frozen, thawed
- 1 1/2 tablespoons olive oil, divided
- 3/4 teaspoon kosher salt, divided
- 2 tablespoons fresh lemon juice
- 2 tablespoons fresh dill, chopped

Instructions

1. Cook the pasta according to the package instructions, drain, and reserve ½ cup of the cooking liquid. Cover the cooked pasta and keep warm.
2. In the meantime, pat dry the shrimp with the paper towels, season with pepper, and ¼ teaspoon of salt.
3. Heat ½ of olive oil in a nonstick skillet over high heat, then add shrimp. Cook for about 3-4 minutes as you stir often until the shrimp is cooked through. Transfer the cooked shrimp to a plate and cover it to keep warm.
4. Reduce the heat to medium-high and add leek to the same skillet along with garlic, remaining ½ teaspoon of salt and the remaining oil. Cook for about 2-3 minutes as you stir often until the leek has become slightly tender.
5. Add the peas to the skillet along with cream, lemon juice, lemon zest and the reserved ½ cup of the cooking liquid. Reduce the heat to medium and simmer for 2-3 minutes until the sauce has slightly thickened. Add in the shrimp and toss well until coated.
6. When through, divide the cooked pasta among the serving bowls and top with the shrimp and sauce evenly. Sprinkle with the chopped fresh dill. Serve immediately and enjoy!

Nutritional info (per serving): 446 calories; 13 g fat; 59 g total carbs; 28 g protein

Pasta Salad with Tomatoes and Eggplant

Prep time: 15 minutes   **Servings:** 4

Ingredients

- 1 tablespoon garlic, minced
- 8 oz. casarecce, fusilli, or penne pasta, uncooked
- 2 teaspoons white wine vinegar
- 8 oz. haricots verts (French green beans), trimmed
- 1/4 cup dry white wine
- 1 tablespoon olive oil
- 6 oz. burrata
- 2 cups Japanese eggplant, chopped
- 1/2 teaspoon kosher salt
- 2 teaspoons fresh thyme, chopped
- 4 cups cherry tomatoes, halved, divided
- 1/2 teaspoon black pepper

Instructions

1. Cook the pasta according to the package instructions. Next, add in the beans 3 minutes before the cooking time is over. Drain and reserve 1 cup of cooking liquid.
2. In the meantime, heat the oil in a skillet over medium-high heat, add in the eggplant. Cook for 4-5 minutes as you stir occasionally until the eggplant has become tender.
3. Add the garlic to the skillet and cook for 1 minute until fragrant, add half of tomatoes. Continue cooking for an additional 2-3 minutes.
4. Add the wine to the skillet as you stir often until most wine has evaporated, then add in pasta and beans. Toss well to combine. If the mixture is too dry, add in a couple tablespoons of the reserved pasta cooking liquid at a time.
5. Stir the remaining tomatoes in the skillet, along with salt and vinegar. Divide the pasta mixture among the serving bowls and top with burrata, pepper, and thyme. Serve and enjoy!

Nutritional info (per serving): 428 calories; 14 g fat; 56 g total carbs; 17 g protein

Balela Salad

Prep time: 15 minutes

Servings: 6-7

Ingredients

- 1/2 cup mint or basil leaves, chopped
- 3 1/2 cups cooked chickpeas
- 1/2 cup parsley leaves, chopped
- 1/2 green bell pepper, cored and chopped
- 1/4 cup green olives, pitted
- 1 jalapeno, chopped
- 1/3 cup Kalamata olives, pitted
- 2 1/2 cups grape tomatoes or cherry tomatoes, whole or cut into halves
- 1/2 cup sun-dried tomatoes
- 3–5 green onions, both white and green parts, chopped

For the Dressing:
- 1 garlic clove, minced
- 4 tablespoons extra virgin olive oil
- 1/2 teaspoon aleppo pepper
- 2 tablespoons white wine vinegar
- 1 teaspoon ground sumac
- 2 tablespoons lemon juice
- Salt and black pepper, to taste

Instructions

1. Add all the salad ingredients to a bowl; mix well.
2. Take another bowl and add all the ingredients for the dressing; mix well.
3. Top the salad with the dressing; toss well until coated; refrigerate for 30 minutes and serve.

Nutritional info (per serving): 288 calories; 7.7 g fat; 48 g total carbs; 10 g protein

Fattoush Salad

Prep time: 20 minutes

Servings: 6

Ingredients

- 1 English cucumber, chopped
- 1 cup fresh mint leaves, chopped
- 2 pita bread loaves, toasted
- 2 cups fresh parsley leaves, stems removed and chopped
- 5 radishes, stems removed, sliced
- 1/2 teaspoon sumac
- 5 green onions (both white and green parts), chopped
- Salt and pepper, to taste
- 5 Roma tomatoes, chopped
- 1 heart Romaine lettuce, chopped

For the Vinaigrette:
- 1 teaspoon ground sumac
- 1/4 teaspoon ground allspice
- 1 1/2 lime, juiced
- 1/4 teaspoon ground cinnamon
- 1/3 cup extra virgin olive oil
- 1/4 teaspoon ground cinnamon
- Salt and pepper, to taste

Instructions

1. Preheat 3 tablespoons of oil in a pan over medium-high heat.
2. Break the toasted bread into small pieces; add these pieces into hot oil and fry them until browned.
3. Add pepper along with ½ teaspoon of sumac and salt; remove from the pan and drain on paper towel.
4. To a bowl, add 1 heart of chopped Romaine lettuce, 5 Roma chopped tomatoes, 5 chopped green onions, 2 cups of chopped fresh parsley leaves, 1 chopped cucumber, and 5 thinly sliced radishes; mix well.
5. **For the vinaigrette:** to a small bowl, add 1/3 cup olive oil, lime juice and all the spices; whisk well. Pour vinaigrette over salad; toss well until coated.
6. Add pita chips. Serve fattoush salad and enjoy!

Nutritional info (per serving): 202 calories; 6 g fat; 35 g total carbs; 5 g protein

Tuna Salad with Dijon Mustard Vinaigrette

Prep time: 15 minutes

Servings: 6-8

Ingredients

For the Dressing:
- 1/3 cup extra virgin olive oil
- 2 1/2 teaspoon Dijon mustard
- 1 lime, zested
- 1/2 teaspoon sumac
- 1 1/2 limes, juiced
- Salt and pepper, to taste

For the Tuna Salad:
- 1/2 red onion, chopped
- 3 cans (5 oz. each) tuna
- 2 1/2 celery stalks, chopped
- ½ cup fresh mint leaves, chopped
- 1/2 English cucumber, chopped
- 1 cup fresh parsley, chopped
- 4–5 whole radishes, stems removed, chopped
- 1/2 cup Kalamata olives, pitted and halved
- 3 green onions, both white and green parts, chopped
- Pita chips/pita pockets, for serving

Instructions

1. To a bowl, combine the lime zest, Dijon mustard, and lime juice; whisk well. Then add 1/2 teaspoon sumac, 1/3 cup oil, 1/2 teaspoon crushed red pepper flakes, pepper and salt; whisk well and set it aside.
2. **For tuna salad:** Take another bowl and combine tuna with 1/2 cup Kalamata olives, 1 cup of chopped fresh parsley, ½ cup of chopped fresh mint leaves and chopped vegetables; mix well.
3. Pour the dressing over the salad; toss well until coated and refrigerate for an hour. Just before serving, toss again.
4. For a sandwich dinner, serve the salad in pita pockets.

Nutritional info (per serving): 604 calories; 10.9 g fat; 12 g total carbs; 67 g protein

White Bean Soup

Prep time: 25 minutes | **Servings:** 6

Ingredients

- 1 teaspoon dried thyme
- 1 tablespoon olive oil
- 1 onion, chopped
- 2 cups baby spinach
- 2 garlic cloves, minced
- 3 cans (15 oz. each) white beans, drained and rinsed
- 1 large carrot, chopped
- ½ teaspoon black pepper
- 1 celery rib, chopped
- 1 teaspoon kosher salt
- 6 cups vegetable broth
- ½ teaspoon oregano
- Fresh parsley, for serving
- Parmesan cheese, grated, for serving

Instructions

1. Preheat the oil in a saucepan over medium heat; add the onion and sauté for about 4-5 minutes until translucent.
2. Then add 1 chopped carrot, ½ teaspoon of oregano, ½ teaspoon black pepper, 1 teaspoon kosher salt, 1 teaspoon dried thyme, 1 chopped celery rib, and 2 minced garlic cloves; cook for another 3-4 minutes.
3. Add 6 cups of vegetable broth along with white beans; boil it lightly; turn the heat down and simmer for approximately 15 minutes.
4. Add 2 cups baby spinach and continue simmering for about 2-4 minutes. Turn the heat off; top with grated cheese and parsley.

Nutritional info (per serving): 249 calories; 3 g fat; 60 g total carbs; 15 g protein

Lentil Soup

Prep time: 50 minutes

Servings: 4

Ingredients

- 1/3 cup celery, chopped
- 3 cups of low sodium chicken broth
- 1 cup red lentils, rinsed
- 1 link chicken andouille sausage, sliced
- 1 tablespoon olive oil
- 1/3 cup carrots, chopped
- 1/3 cup onions, chopped

Instructions

1. In a soup pot, preheat the oil over medium heat. Add 1/3 cup chopped celery, 1/3 cup chopped carrots, and 1/3 cup chopped onions; cook until caramelize for about 4-5 minutes.
2. Add the sausage, along with rinsed red lentils; stir well. Add the chicken broth; reduce the heat and cover the pot.
3. Cook the lentils for about 40-45 minutes. Serve and enjoy!

Nutritional info (per serving): 504 calories; 12 g fat; 34 g total carbs; 64 g protein

Vegetable Soup

Prep time: 40 minutes

Servings: 6

Ingredients

- 2 garlic cloves, minced
- 1 cup fresh baby spinach, stems removed and chopped
- 1 tablespoon olive oil
- ½ cup small shell pasta
- 2 carrots, diced
- 1 teaspoon dried oregano
- 2 celery stalks, diced
- 15 oz. can cannellini beans, drained and rinsed
- ½ cup yellow onion, diced
- 32 ounce vegetable broth
- 2 small zucchini, diced
- 28 oz. can crushed tomatoes

Instructions

1. Preheat the olive oil in a pan over medium heat.
2. Add the onion, zucchini, carrots, garlic, and celery stalks; sauté for about 5 minutes, until tender.
3. Then add the crushed tomatoes along with vegetable broth; increase the heat and boil it lightly.
4. Turn the heat down; add 1 teaspoon dried oregano, along with the cannellini beans; simmer uncovered for approximately 20 minutes.
5. Add and cook ½ cup small shell pasta for 7-8 minutes. Stir in 1 cup fresh baby spinach; cook further for a minute.
6. Transfer to a serving bowl and enjoy!

Nutritional info (per serving): 118 calories; 4.8 g fat; 15 g total carbs; 6 g protein

Mediterranean Chicken Soup

Prep time: 45 minutes   **Servings:** 4-6

Ingredients

- 2 onions, diced
- 2 garlic cloves, minced
- 8 cups chickens stock
- Basil or parsley, chopped, for serving
- 8 tomatoes, diced
- 3 bell peppers, diced
- 3 zucchini, diced
- 2 tablespoons olive oil
- 5 oz. concentrated tomato puree
- 4 garlic cloves, diced
- 3 ½ oz. capers
- Salt, pepper, to taste

Instructions

1. Boil the chicken stock. Add the tomato puree, bell peppers, and tomatoes; boil for 10 minutes.
2. Add the capers with the zucchini; boil again for 10 minutes.
3. In the meantime, preheat the olive oil in a pan. Add the onions and garlic, sauté for about 5 minutes.
4. Now add the sautéed garlic and the onion in the soup and boil for 10 minutes more.
5. At the end, serve the soup with parsley and basil.

Nutritional info (per serving): 265 calories; 7.8 g fat; 23 g total carbs; 5 g protein

Lemony Escarole Soup

Prep time: 55 minutes   **Servings:** 6

Ingredients

- 4 sprigs lemon-thyme and 4 sprigs parsley, tied in a bundle with twine
- 3 tablespoons olive oil
- 3 cups Yukon gold potatoes, chopped
- 1 cup dried ditalini pasta, cooked and drained
- 1 onion, chopped
- 2 tablespoons lemon juice
- 2 celery ribs, chopped
- 1 lemon, zested
- 4 garlic cloves, chopped
- 8 cups escarole, chopped
- ½ cup white wine or sherry
- 32-ounce container + 2 cups low-sodium chicken broth
- 1 can (15 oz.) chickpeas, drained
- Parsley, chopped, for serving
- Feta cheese, for serving

Instructions

1. In a soup pot, heat 3 tablespoons of olive oil. Add 3 cups of chopped Yukon gold potatoes and season with pepper and salt; cook for 5 minutes. Then add 4 minced cloves of garlic, along with 1 chopped onion; season with pepper and salt again. Cover the pot and steam for 5 minutes.
2. Deglaze the pot with ½ cup white wine or sherry; cook for a minute.
3. Add the chickpeas to the herb bundle, low-sodium chicken broth, and a cup of water. Boil it lightly and then simmer for about 7-8 minutes, until potatoes are tender.
4. Add handful of chopped escarole into the soup and cook until wilted.
5. In the end, add lemon zest, two tablespoons lemon juice, and 1 cup dried cooked ditalini pasta.
6. Garnish the soup with chopped parsley and feta cheese. Serve and enjoy!

Nutritional info (per serving): 356 calories; 16.8 g fat; 44 g total carbs; 12 g protein

Dinner

Couscous with Tuna and Pepperoncini

Prep time: 15 minutes   **Servings:** 4

Ingredients

- 1 cup chicken broth or water
- ¾ teaspoon salt
- 1¼ cups couscous
- ⅓ cup fresh parsley, chopped
- 1 lemon, quartered
- 2 cans (5 0z each) oil packed tuna
- 1 pint cherry tomatoes, halved
- Extra-virgin olive oil (for serving)
- ½ cup pepperoncini, sliced
- ¼ cup capers
- Salt, pepper, to taste

Instructions

1. Add 1 cup chicken broth or water to a small pot and boil it. Turn the heat off, stir in 1¼ cups of couscous, and cover it. Let it boil for 10 minutes.
2. In the meantime, take another bowl and add 1 pint of halved cherry tomatoes, ½ cup of sliced pepperoncini, ¼ cup capers, ⅓ cup fresh chopped parsley, and oil packed tuna; toss well.
3. Fluff the couscous with a fork. Season with pepper and salt; drizzle with olive oil.
4. Top with the mixture of tuna and serve your meal with lemon wedges.

Nutritional info (per serving): 226 calories; 10 g fat; 44 g total carbs; 22 g protein

Mediterranean Cod

Prep time: 30 minutes　　　　　**Servings:** 4

Ingredients

- 1/2 cup water
- 1 teaspoon orange zest
- 2 tablespoons olive oil
- 1 onion, sliced
- 1/4 teaspoon black pepper
- 2 cups fennel, sliced
- 1/8 teaspoon salt
- 3 cloves garlic, chopped
- 1 lb. cod, cut into 4 pieces
- 1 can (14.5 oz.) diced tomato
- 1 cup oil cured black olives
- 1 cup fresh tomatoes, diced
- 2 teaspoons fresh oregano
- 2 cups kale, shredded
- Pinch of red pepper, crushed

Instructions

1. Preheat the olive oil in a skillet and cook the garlic, fennel, and onion over medium heat, for about 7-8 minutes. Season with ¼ teaspoon of each pepper and salt.
2. Add 1 cup fresh diced tomatoes, 2 cups of shredded kale, 1/2 cup water, and diced tomatoes; cook for about 12 minutes.
3. Add 2 teaspoons fresh oregano, black olives, and a pinch of crushed red pepper.
4. Prepare the fish, season with 1/4 teaspoon of fennel seeds, 1 teaspoon of orange zest, 1/4 teaspoon black pepper, and 1/8 teaspoon salt.
5. Add the fish to the kale tomato mixture and cover the pot; cook for approximately 10 minutes.
6. Serve warm and enjoy!

Nutritional info (per serving): 235 calories; 13 g fat; 12 g total carbs; 23 g protein

Shrimp with Pineapple Rice

Prep time: 35-45 minutes   **Servings:** 4-5

Ingredients

- 1/2 teaspoon garlic powder
- 2 tablespoons cilantro, chopped
- 1 cup water
- 1 cup basmati rice
- 1/2 cup pineapple juice
- 1 tablespoon lime juice
- 1 cup pineapple chunks, drained
- 1 tablespoon maple syrup
- 1 tablespoon butter
- 1/2 teaspoon salt
- 1/4 teaspoon red pepper, crushed
- 1/2 teaspoon onion powder
- 1 teaspoon curry powder

For the Shrimp:
- 4 cups shrimp
- Green onions, chopped
- 2 garlic cloves, minced
- 2 1/4 teaspoon Caribbean jerk seasoning
- 2 tablespoons butter

Instructions

1. Add pineapple juice, butter, water, pineapple chunks, curry powder, onion powder, garlic powder, maple syrup, 1/2 teaspoon salt, 1 tablespoon lime juice, and 1/4 teaspoon crushed red pepper in a medium sized pot; add in 1 cup of basmati rice; bring to a boil over medium heat.
2. Turn the heat down; cover and simmer until rice becomes soft and water is adsorbed, for about 20 minutes.
3. Turn the heat off; and let the rice rest 10 minutes. Fluff the rice with a fork and then stir into the cilantro.
4. **For the shrimp:** Add 2 tablespoons butter to a pan and melt it over medium heat. Add 2 garlic cloves and sauté until fragrant for about 1-2 minutes.
5. Turn the heat down. Next, stir in 2 1/4 teaspoons Caribbean jerk seasoning, and the shrimp.
6. Cook until the shrimp becomes pink, for about 2/3 minutes. Turn the heat off; toss with green onions, and serve the shrimp over cooked rice. Enjoy!

Nutritional info (per serving): 428 calories; 14 g fat; 56 g total carbs; 17 g protein

Lemon Chicken with Asparagus

Prep time: 10 minutes

Servings: 3-4

Ingredients

- 1 lb. boneless skinless chicken breasts
- 2 tablespoons honey + 2 tablespoons butter
- 1/4 cup flour
- 2 lemons, sliced
- 1/2 teaspoon salt, pepper to taste
- 1 teaspoon lemon pepper seasoning
- 1–2 cups asparagus, chopped
- 2 tablespoons butter

Instructions

1. Cut the chicken breast in half horizontally. In a shallow dish, mix 1/4 cup flour and salt and pepper to taste; toss the chicken breast until coated.
2. To a skillet, add 2 tablespoons of butter and melt over medium heat. Then add the coated chicken breast and cook each side for about 4-5 minutes, sprinkling both sides with lemon pepper.
3. Once chicken is completely cooked through and is golden brown, transfer it to a plate.

For Asparagus and Lemons:
1. To the pan, add 1–2 cups chopped asparagus; sauté until bright green for a few minutes.
2. Remove from the pan and keep it aside. Place the slices of lemon to the bottom of the pan and cook each side until caramelized, for a few minutes without stirring.
3. Add a bit of butter along with the lemon slices. Take the lemons out of the pan and put them aside.
4. Serve the chicken with the asparagus and enjoy!

Nutritional info (per serving): 232 calories; 9 g fat; 10.4 g total carbs; 27.5 g protein

Cilantro Lime Chicken

Prep time: 12 minutes   **Servings:** 4

Ingredients

- 2 tablespoons olive oil
- 1/4 teaspoon salt
- 1.5 lb. boneless chicken breast
- 1/2 teaspoon ground cumin
- 1/4 cup lime juice
- 1/4 cup fresh cilantro

For Avocado Salsa:
- 1/2 tablespoon red wine vinegar
- Salt, to taste
- 4 avocados, diced
- 1 garlic clove, minced
- 1/2 cup fresh cilantro, diced
- 1/2 teaspoon red pepper flakes
- 3 tablespoons lime juice

Instructions

1. Add cilantro, lime juice, 1/2 teaspoon ground cumin, 2 tablespoons olive oil, and salt to a bowl; whisk well.
2. Add the marinade and chicken breast to a large Ziploc bag; marinate for about 15 minutes.
3. Preheat the grill to 400°F. Grill the chicken until it's no longer pink, for about 5-7 minutes per side. Remove from the grill.
4. **For avocado salsa:** add lime juice, cilantro, 1/2 tablespoon red wine vinegar, 1/2 teaspoon red pepper flakes, 1 minced clove of garlic, salt, and 4 diced avocados to a blender; process well until smooth.
5. Serve and enjoy!

Nutritional info (per serving): 317 calories; 22 g fat; 11 g total carbs; 24 g protein

Shrimp And Leek Spaghetti

Prep time: 20 minutes   **Servings:** 4

Ingredients

- 1 lb. peeled, deveined raw shrimp
- 8 oz. uncooked whole-grain spaghetti
- 1 tablespoon garlic, chopped
- 2 cups leek, chopped
- 1 ½ tablespoons olive oil
- ¼ cup heavy cream
- 2 cups frozen baby sweet peas
- 2 tablespoons dill, chopped
- 2 teaspoons lemon zest
- 2 tablespoons lemon juice
- ½ teaspoon black pepper
- ¾ teaspoon kosher salt

Instructions

1. Cook the pasta according to the package instructions. Drain and reserve ½ cup cooking liquid. Cover the pasta.
2. Pat dry the shrimp and season with pepper and ¼ teaspoon salt.
3. Heat half of the oil in a skillet over high heat. Add shrimp and cook for 4 minutes, stirring often. Transfer to a plate and cover.
4. Reduce the heat to medium high. Add garlic, leek, ½ teaspoon salt, and the remaining oil. Cook for 3 minutes, stirring often.
5. Add cream, peas, lemon zest, lemon juice, and the reserved liquid. Reduce the heat to medium and cook for 3 minutes. Add the shrimp to the skillet and toss well.
6. Add the pasta evenly to 4 bowls. Add the sauce and the shrimp on top.
7. Add dill and serve.

Nutritional info (per serving): 446 calories; 13 g fat; 59 g total carbs; 28 g protein

Panko Salmon With Snap Peas

Prep time: 20 minutes

Servings: 4

Ingredients

- 1 ½ tablespoons canola mayonnaise
- 1 ½ tablespoons Dijon mustard
- 4 (6 oz.) skinless salmon fillets
- 1 tablespoon tarragon, chopped
- ½ cup whole-wheat panko
- 2 tablespoons olive oil
- 2 teaspoons lemon rind, grated
- 2 ½ cups sugar snap peas, trimmed
- 2 teaspoons lemon juice
- 1/3 cup shallots, sliced
- ¾ teaspoon salt
- ½ teaspoon black pepper

Instructions

1. Mix mayonnaise, mustard, ½ teaspoon salt, and ¼ teaspoon pepper in a bowl. Add the mustard mixture evenly over the fillets.
2. Mix 1 ½ teaspoons tarragon, panko, and 1 teaspoon lemon rind in a bowl. Add the panko mixture over the fillets.
3. Heat 1 tablespoon oil in a skillet over medium heat. Add fillets to the skillet, panko side down. Cook for 4 minutes, turn, and cook for 4 more minutes. Remove the fillets from the pan.
4. Increase the heat to medium high and add the remaining oil to the pan.
5. Add the shallots with the snap peas and cook for 3 minutes, stirring occasionally.
6. Add the remaining salt, pepper, 1 ½ teaspoons tarragon, 1 teaspoon lemon rind, and juice to the pan. Cook for 2 minutes.
7. Once cooked, serve with the fillets.

Nutritional info (per serving): 387 calories; 18 g fat; 13 g total carbs; 39 g protein

Gnocchi With Spinach And Pepper Sauce

Prep time: 20 minutes

Servings: 5

Ingredients

- 5 oz. baby spinach
- 16 oz. whole-wheat potato gnocchi
- 3 tablespoons olive oil
- 1 ½ oz. Manchego cheese, grated
- ¼ cup smoked almonds
- ½ cup jarred roasted red peppers, chopped
- 1 garlic clove
- 1 plum tomato, chopped
- 2 tablespoons sherry vinegar
- 1 baguette slice, torn
- ½ teaspoon paprika
- ¼ teaspoon red pepper, crushed

Instructions

1. Cook the gnocchi according to package instructions. Drain and return to the pan.
2. Add ¼ cup cheese, spinach, and 1 tablespoon oil and cook for 3 minutes. Toss to combine.
3. Add almonds, red peppers, baguette, tomato, garlic, vinegar, red pepper, paprika, and the remaining 2 tablespoons olive oil to a blender and blend for 1 minute.
4. Divide the gnocchi mixture among 5 bowls. Add sauce and the remaining 2 tablespoons cheese evenly. Finally, serve.

Nutritional info (per serving): 324 calories; 16 g fat; 34 g total carbs; 9 g protein

Chicken And Bulgur Salad With Peaches

Prep time: 20 minutes

Servings: 4

Ingredients

- 2/3 cup bulgur
- 1 1/3 cups water
- 4 cups packed arugula
- 1 lb. chicken breast cutlets
- 2 cups cherry tomatoes, halved
- 2 tablespoons rice vinegar
- 3 tablespoons olive oil
- 2 cups peaches, sliced
- 1 teaspoon kosher salt
- ½ teaspoon black pepper
- cooking spray

Instructions

1. Add bulgur, 1 1/3 cups water to a pan, and boil over high heat. Reduce the heat to medium low, cover and cook for 10 minutes. Drain and rinse in cold water. Drain well and pat dry.
2. Heat a grill pan over high heat and grease with cooking spray.
3. Season the chicken with ½ teaspoon salt and pepper. Grill chicken for 7 minutes, stirring occasionally. Place on a cutting board and let it sit for 3 minutes. Slice against the grain into strips.
4. Add the arugula, bulgur, tomatoes, and peaches to a bowl.
5. Add the remaining oil, salt, and vinegar and toss well to coat.
6. Divide the mixture among 4 bowls. Add the chicken evenly and serve.

Nutritional info (per serving): 364 calories; 14 g fat; 30 g total carbs; 31 g protein

Greek Turkey Burgers

Prep time: 20 minutes

Servings: 4

Ingredients

- ¼ cup canola mayonnaise
- 1 lb. 93% lean ground turkey
- 1 teaspoon ground cumin
- 2 teaspoons dried oregano
- 1/3 cup whole-wheat Greek yogurt
- 1 tablespoon lemon juice
- 2 cups arugula
- 1/3 cup Kalamata olives, chopped
- 4 whole-wheat hamburger buns
- ½ cup red onion, thinly sliced
- ½ cup cucumber, sliced
- ¼ teaspoon kosher salt
- ¼ teaspoon black pepper

Instructions

1. Mix the mayo, turkey, cumin, oregano, salt, and 1/8 teaspoon pepper. Next, shape the mixture into 4 patties.
2. Heat a skillet over high heat. Grease the skillet with cooking spray.
3. Add turkey patties and cook for 5 minutes per side.
4. Mix lemon juice, yogurt, olives, and the remaining 1/8 teaspoon pepper to a bowl.
5. Spread the yogurt mixture evenly on cut sides of top and bottom buns. Divide arugula among bottom halves of the buns. Top with patties, red onion, and cucumber.
6. Cover with buns and serve.

Nutritional info (per serving): 375 calories; 17 g fat; 28 g total carbs; 29 g protein

Orange Balsamic Lamb Chops

Prep time: 20 minutes

Servings: 4

Ingredients

- 1 tablespoon orange juice
- 4 teaspoons olive oil
- 2 teaspoons orange rind, grated
- 3 tablespoons balsamic vinegar
- 8 (4 oz.) lamb rib chops, trimmed
- 1 teaspoon kosher salt
- ½ teaspoon pepper
- cooking spray

Instructions

1. Mix rind, 1 tablespoon olive oil, and juice in a Ziploc bag.
2. Add the lamb to the bag and coat well. Let it sit for 10 minutes. Remove lamb from the bag and season well.
3. Heat a grill pan over medium high heat and grease with cooking spray. Add lamb to the pan and cook for 2 minutes per side.
4. Add vinegar to a skillet over medium high heat and bring to boil. Cook for 3 minutes.
5. Add vinegar and the remaining oil over the lamb and serve.

Nutritional info (per serving): 226 calories; 12 g fat; 2 g total carbs; 25 g protein

Seared Mediterranean Tuna Steaks

Prep time: 20 minutes

Servings: 4

Ingredients

- 4 (6 oz.) yellow fin tuna steaks, ¾ inch thick
- ½ teaspoon ground coriander
- 1 ½ cups seeded tomato, chopped
- ¼ cup green onions, chopped
- 3 tablespoons parsley, chopped
- 1 tablespoon lemon juice
- 12 Kalamata olives, chopped and pitted
- 1 tablespoon olive oil
- 1 tablespoon capers, drained
- ½ teaspoon bottled minced garlic
- ½ teaspoon salt
- 1/8 teaspoon pepper
- cooking spray

Instructions

1. Add ¼ teaspoon salt, pepper and coriander over fish.
2. Heat a skillet over medium high heat. Grease the pan with cooking spray. Add the fish to the pan and cook for 4 minutes per side.
3. Mix the tomato, ¼ teaspoon salt, and the remaining ingredients in a bowl.
4. Add the tomato mixture over the fish and serve.

Nutritional info (per serving): 268 calories; 8.5 g fat; 5.5 g total carbs; 41 g protein

Greek Style Scampi

Prep time: 40 minutes

Servings: 4

Ingredients

- 4 garlic cloves, minced
- 1 tablespoon olive oil
- 1 ¼ lbs. large shrimp, peeled, and deveined
- ¼ cup parsley, chopped
- 4 (14 ½ oz.) cans whole, peeled tomatoes, drained and chopped
- 1 ½ tablespoons lemon juice
- ¾ cup crumbled feta cheese
- 1/8 teaspoon salt
- ¼ teaspoon black pepper
- 8 ounces pasta, cooked and drained

Instructions

1. Preheat the oven to 400 F.
2. Heat a Dutch oven over medium heat. Add oil to the pan and coat well.
3. Add the garlic, cook, and stir for 30 seconds.
4. Add 2 tablespoons parsley, tomatoes, and salt. Reduce the heat and cook for 7 minutes.
5. Add the shrimp and cook for 5 minutes.
6. Add the mixture to a baking dish. Add cheese on top. Bake for 10 minutes.
7. Once cooked, add the remaining 2 tablespoons parsley, pepper, and lemon juice on top and serve.

Nutritional info (per serving): 301 calories; 10.5 g fat; 13 g total carbs; 34 g protein

Couscous With Artichokes Feta And Sun Dried Tomatoes

Prep time: 30 minutes

Servings: 6 cups

Ingredients

- ½ cup sun-dried tomatoes
- 2 1/3 cups water
- 1 ¾ cups uncooked Israeli couscous
- 14 ½ oz. can vegetable broth
- ½ cup feta cheese, crumbled
- 3 cups cooked chicken breasts, chopped
- 1 cup parsley, chopped
- 2 (6 oz.) jars marinated artichoke hearts, undrained
- ¼ teaspoon black pepper

Instructions

1. Add 2 cups water and tomatoes into a heat proof bowl. Microwave for 3 minutes on high, cover, and let sit for 10 minutes. Drain, chop, and set aside.
2. Add the vegetable broth and 1/3 cup water to a pan and bring to boil.
3. Add the couscous. Cover, reduce the heat, and cook for 8 minutes.
4. Once cooked, remove from the heat, add in the tomatoes, the remaining ingredients, and serve.

Nutritional info (per serving): 419 calories; 14 g fat; 42.5 g total carbs; 30 g protein

Pasta With Sun Dried Tomato Pesto And Feta Cheese

Prep time: 20 minutes **Servings:** 4

Ingredients

- ¾ cup oil-packed sun-dried tomato halves, drained
- 2 tablespoons slivered almonds
- ¼ cup loosely packed basil leaves
- 9 oz. pack refrigerated fresh linguine
- 1 tablespoon garlic, minced
- 2 tablespoon Parmesan cheese, shredded
- ½ cup feta cheese, crumbled
- ½ teaspoon salt
- ¼ teaspoon black pepper

Instructions

1. Cook the pasta according to package instructions. Drain with a sieve and reserve 1 cup liquid. Return pasta to the pan.
2. Add tomatoes, basil, almonds, parmesan, garlic, salt, and pepper to a blender and blend until chopped.
3. Mix the tomato mixture, reserved 1 cup liquid, and stir with a whisk. Add this to pasta and toss to coat well.
4. Add feta and serve.

Nutritional info (per serving): 300 calories; 10 g fat; 42 g total carbs; 12 g protein

Mussels In Spicy Tomato Sauce

Prep time: 15 minutes   **Servings:** 4

Ingredients

- 1 oz. prosciutto, diced
- 1 tablespoon olive oil
- 2 tablespoons shallot, chopped
- 1 tablespoon butter
- ½ teaspoon red pepper, crushed
- 2 teaspoons garlic, chopped
- 1 cup san Marzano tomatoes, chopped
- 1 teaspoon granulated sugar
- ½ cup dry white wine
- 2 lbs. mussels, scrubbed and debearded
- 2 tablespoons parsley, chopped
- 8 ½ oz. whole-wheat baguette slices, toasted
- 3/8 teaspoon kosher salt
- lemon wedges

Instructions

1. Heat butter and olive oil in a Dutch oven over medium high for 1 minute.
2. Add prosciutto, shallot and cook for 5 minutes, stirring occasionally.
3. Add red pepper and garlic. Then cook for 1 minute, stirring.
4. Add sugar, tomatoes, wine, and salt. Next, bring to a simmer.
5. Add the mussels to the sauce; cover and cook for 5 minutes.
6. Add 1 tablespoon parsley. Toss and add into 4 bowls.
7. Add the remaining parsley on top and serve with bread.

Nutritional info (per serving): 376 calories; 10 g fat; 26 g total carbs; 38 g protein

Easy Stuffed Peppers

Prep time: 15 minutes

Servings: 4

Ingredients

- 2 tablespoon pesto sauce
- 4 red peppers
- 1 lb. cooked tomato rice
- 2 cups goat cheese, sliced
- handful black olives, pitted

Instructions

1. Cut the top of the red peppers and scoop out the seeds. Place the peppers on the plate, cut side up, and microwave for 6 minutes on high.
2. Mix the rice with pesto with a handful of black olives, and 1 3/8 cup cheese. Add this mixture on the peppers and top with the remaining cheese. Cook for 10 minutes.
3. Serve.

Nutritional info (per serving): 387 calories; 17 g fat; 46 g total carbs; 15 g protein

Mediterranean Vegetables With Lamb

Prep time: 45 minutes

Servings: 4

Ingredients

- 2 large courgettes, cut into chunks
- 1 tablespoon olive oil
- ½ teaspoon ground cumin, paprika and ground coriander
- ½ lb. lean lamb fillet, fat trimmed ,and thinly sliced
- 1 3/8 cup shallot, halved
- 1 garlic clove, sliced
- 1 red, 1 yellow and 1 orange pepper, cut into chunks
- 5 oz. veggie stock
- ½ lb. cherry tomatoes
- handful coriander leaves, chopped

Instructions

1. Heat the oil in a frying pan. Cook the shallots and lamb over high heat for 3 minutes.
2. Add the courgettes and stir fry for 4 minutes.
3. Add the spices and toss well.
4. Add the garlic and peppers. Reduce the heat and cook for 5 minutes over moderate heat.
5. Add the stock and coat well
6. Add the tomatoes, season, cover, and simmer for 15 minutes, stirring occasionally.
7. Add coriander and serve.

Nutritional info (per serving): 192 calories; 9 g fat; 11 g total carbs; 17 g protein

Mediterranean Chicken Tray Bake

Prep time: 50 minutes   **Servings:** 4

Ingredients

- 2 teaspoon olive oil
- 2 red peppers, deseeded and cut into chunks
- 4 skin-on chicken breasts
- 1 red onion, cut into wedges
- ¾ cup full-fat garlic and herb soft cheese
- ½ lb. cherry tomatoes
- handful black olives
- 400g baby potatoes, larger ones cut in half

Instructions

1. Heat the oven to 395 F.
2. Mix the peppers and onion on a baking tray. Next, add half of the oil. Place in the oven and bake for 10 minutes on the top rack.
3. Make a pocket between the skin and flesh of each chicken breast and add equal amounts of cheese under the skin. Smooth the skin back down, brush with the remaining oil, season, and add to the baking tray.
4. Add the olives and tomatoes.
5. Bake in the oven for 30 minutes.
6. Once cooked, serve.

Nutritional info (per serving): 401 calories; 21 g fat; 9 g total carbs; 45 g protein

Desserts

Tiramisu

Prep time: 40 minutes   **Servings:** 6-8

Ingredients

- 1 cup sugar
- 6 egg yolks
- 1 ¾ cup heavy whipping cream
- 1 ¼ cup mascarpone cheese
- 2 7 oz. pack Italian Lady fingers
- 1 cup cold espresso
- 1 oz. unsweetened cocoa

Instructions

1. Mix sugar and egg yolks in a bowl placed over boiling water. Whisk until smooth.
2. Remove from the heat and whip the yolks until thick. Cool and mix in the mascarpone cheese until well combined.
3. Whip the cream in a separate bowl with a mixer. Fold the cream into the mascarpone mixture and set aside.
4. Soak the ladyfingers in cold espresso and arrange them on a baking dish. Add half of the mascarpone mixture over the ladyfingers. Repeat the process with another layer of ladyfingers. Add another layer of the tiramisu cream. Refrigerate for 4 hours.
5. Dust with cocoa and serve.

Nutritional info (per serving): 490 calories; 34 g fat; 37 g total carbs; 5 g protein

Italian Apple Olive Oil Cake

Prep time: 1 hour

Servings: 8-10

Ingredients

- 3 cups all-purpose flour
- 2 apples, peeled and chopped
- ½ teaspoon ground nutmeg
- ½ teaspoon ground cinnamon
- 1 teaspoon baking soda
- 1 teaspoon baking powder
- 1 cup olive oil
- 1 cup sugar
- 2 eggs
- 2/3 cup gold raisins
- Confectioner's sugar
- Orange juice

Instructions

1. Preheat the oven to 350 F.
2. Add the chopped apples to a bowl with orange juice. Toss and coat well. Sift the flour, nutmeg, cinnamon, baking powder, and baking soda in a bowl and set aside.
3. Add the olive oil and sugar to a mixer bowl and beat well. Add the eggs, one at a time, and mix for 2 more minutes.
4. Make a well in the middle of the flour mixture. Add the wet mixture into it. Stir until well blended.
5. Soak raisins in warm water for 15 minutes. Drain completely and then drain the apples. Add the apples and raisins to the batter and mix with a spoon.
6. Line a 9" cake pan with parchment paper. Add the batter to the pan. Bake for 45 minutes. Cool completely in the pan. Remove to a serving dish and dust with confectioner's sugar. Serve.

Nutritional info (per serving): 412 calories; 24 g fat; 44 g total carbs; 6 g protein

Greek Cheesecake with Yogurt

Prep time: 20 minutes

Servings: 12

Ingredients

- 1 teaspoon vanilla extract
- 9 oz. digestive biscuits
- 3 ½ oz. butter, melted
- 5 oz. Greek yogurt
- 16 oz. cream cheese
- 2 tablespoons honey
- 4 oz. icing sugar
- 280 ml double cream
- 1 cup any jam

Instructions

1. Add the biscuits to a blender and pulse until crumbled. Transfer the crumbs to a bowl and add the melted butter. Mix well until the crumbs are well coated. Add to the pan and press into the bottom. Refrigerate.
2. Add Greek yogurt, cream cheese, icing sugar, vanilla, and honey to a bowl. Beat with a mixer until smooth. Add the double cream and beat until well combined.
3. Add the mixture onto the biscuit crust and top the cheesecake with jam. Refrigerate overnight. Serve.

Nutritional info (per serving): 402 calories; 27 g fat; 36.1 g total carbs; 5.2 g protein

Greek Yogurt and Honey Walnuts

Prep time: 10 minutes

Servings: 6

Ingredients

- ½ cup honey
- 2 ½ cups strained Greek yogurt
- 1 cup walnuts
- ¾ teaspoon vanilla extract
- Cinnamon powder

Instructions

1. Preheat oven to 375 F.
2. Add the walnuts in a single layer onto the baking sheet. Toast for 8 minutes. Transfer the walnuts to a bowl. Add honey and stir to coat well. Cool down for 2 minutes.
3. Mix vanilla extract and Greek yogurt and divide among bowls. Add the honey-walnut mixture over the yogurt and add cinnamon powder on top. Serve.

Nutritional info (per serving): 284 calories; 16 g fat; 26.7 g total carbs; 11.8 g protein

Chocolate Brownies

Prep time: 35 minutes   **Servings:** 16

Ingredients

- 6 oz. tahini
- 2 oz. cognac
- 3 orange juices
- 5 ½ oz. all-purpose flour
- 7 oz. dark couverture chocolate
- ½ teaspoon baking powder
- 5 oz. icing sugar
- 1 orange, zested
- 3 ½ oz. walnuts, chopped

Instructions

1. Melt half of the chocolate. Set aside for 5 minutes.
2. Add the orange juice, tahini, and cognac to a bowl and whisk to combine. Add melted chocolate and mix again. Add the sugar, baking powder and flour and stir with a spoon until smooth. Add the chopped walnuts and remaining chocolate and stir again.
3. Preheat the oven to 375 F and line a square baking pan with parchment paper and grease with vegetable oil. Dust with cocoa powder and discard excess cocoa. Add the brownie mixture to the pan and spread evenly.
4. Bake the brownies for 25 minutes. Set aside and cool for 30 minutes. Serve.

Nutritional info (per serving): 251 calories; 13.9 g fat; 0 g total carbs; 4.4 g protein

Peach Nectarine Mango Crumble

Prep time: 45 minutes

Servings: 6

Ingredients

- 2 peaches
- 4 nectarines
- ¼ cup brown sugar
- ½ mango
- 1 cup salted butter
- 1 cup flour
- 8 speculoos cookies, crushed

Instructions

1. Cut all the fruits into small squares and add to a baking dish. Preheat the oven to 350 F.
2. Mix the flour, sugar, and cookie crumbs in a bowl. Add butter and mix with hands to make a base. Add this mixture to the fruits. Next, spread evenly.
3. Bake for 30 minutes. Serve.

Nutritional info (per serving): 454 calories; 25.4 g fat; 55 g total carbs; 5 g protein

Cherry Clafoutis

Prep time: 45 minutes   **Servings:** 8

Ingredients

- ½ cup all-purpose flour
- 1 ¼ lbs. sweet cherries
- 3 eggs
- 1 teaspoon vanilla extract
- 1/8 teaspoon almond extract
- 1 1/3 cup whole milk
- ½ cup + 3 tablespoons sugar
- Butter, softened

Instructions

1. Preheat the oven to 375 F. Next, add butter to a shallow baking dish and grease the dish well.
2. Stem and pit the cherries and lay them in a single layer in the baking dish. Mix the flour, eggs, vanilla and almond extract, milk, and ½ cup sugar in a blender, process until smooth.
3. Add the batter over the cherries and sprinkle with 3 tablespoons sugar. Bake the clafoutis for 45 minutes. Serve.

Nutritional info (per serving): 184 calories; 5.1 g fat; 29 g total carbs; 6 g protein

Blood Orange Olive Oil Cake

Prep time: 1 hour

Servings: 8

Ingredients

- 1 ¼ cup all-purpose flour
- 1 blood orange
- 2 teaspoons baking powder
- ½ cup medium-grind oatmeal
- ¼ teaspoon baking soda
- ½ cup whole-milk plain yogurt
- 3 eggs
- 2/3 cup + 2 tablespoons granulated sugar
- ½ cup olive oil
- ¼ teaspoon fine sea salt
- Cooking spray

Instructions

1. Place a rack in the center of the oven and preheat the oven to 350 F. Grease the loaf pan with cooking spray and set aside.
2. Peel the orange zest and cut into thin strips. Set aside. Juice the orange and set ¼ cup of juice aside.
3. Whisk the cornmeal, flour, baking soda, powder, and salt in a bowl and set aside. Whisk 2/3 cup sugar and ¼ cup blood orange juice in a bowl. Whisk in the eggs, yogurt and olive oil. Whisk flour mixture into the wet ingredients and mix until just combined. Add zest strips.
4. Add batter to the prepared pan. Add 2 tablespoons sugar and blood orange slices and bake for 1 hour.
5. Let the cake cool on the wire rack for 20 minutes. Serve.

Nutritional info (per serving): 301 calories; 18 g fat; 29 g total carbs; 6 g protein

Gluten Free Lemon Cake

Prep time: 40 minutes   **Servings:** 8

Ingredients

- ¾ cup polenta
- 2 cups almond flour
- 7 oz. unsalted butter
- 1 ½ teaspoons baking powder
- 3 eggs
- 1 cup granulated sugar
- ½ teaspoon vanilla extract
- 2 lemons zest
- ¼ teaspoon salt
- 3 tablespoons lemon juice
- ½ cup powdered sugar

Instructions

1. Place a rack in the center of the oven and heat it to 350 F. Line a spring-form pan with parchment paper. Coat the sides of the pan with butter and set aside.
2. Add the polenta, almond flour, baking powder, and salt to a bowl and whisk to combine. Set aside.
3. Add the sugar and butter to a bowl of a stand mixer. Beat on medium speed for 3 minutes. Add 1/3 cup almond flour mixture and beat well. Beat in 1 egg until mixed well. Add the remaining eggs and almond flour and mix until smooth. Stop the mixer to scrape the sides of the bowl from time to time.
4. Add the vanilla extract and lemon zest and beat until mixed well. Add the batter to the pan in a single layer. Bake for 40 minutes. Place the pan on the wire rack.
5. Add lemon juice and powdered sugar to the pan placed over low heat and cook until the sugar is dissolved. Remove from the heat.
6. Poke holes in the cake with a toothpick. Add the syrup on top of the cake and spread evenly. Let cool for 1 ½ hours. Serve.

Nutritional info (per serving): 274 calories; 17.6 g fat; 25 g total carbs; 5 g protein

Yogurt and Honey Olive Oil Cake

Prep time: 45 minutes   **Servings:** 8

Ingredients

- 1 cup whole Greek yogurt
- 2/3 cup honey
- 2/3 cup olive oil
- 3 eggs
- 1 tablespoon thyme leaves, chopped
- 1 teaspoon lemon zest, grated
- ½ teaspoon baking powder
- 1 ½ cups all-purpose flour
- ½ teaspoon baking soda
- ¼ teaspoon salt

Instructions

1. Place a rack in the center of the oven and preheat it to 325 F.
2. Grease a 9" round cake pan with cooking spray and line with parchment paper. Grease again.
3. Whisk the olive oil, honey, yogurt, thyme, and lemon zest in a bowl. Add the eggs one at a time and whisk well. Add the baking powder, flour, baking soda, and salt. Stir the batter until smooth.
4. Add the batter to the cake pan and spread evenly. Bake for 45 minutes. Transfer the cake to a cooling rack and cool for 10 minutes. Flip the cake onto a plate. Serve.

Nutritional info (per serving): 399 calories; 22.9 g fat; 43 g total carbs; 7 g protein

Snacks

Greek Yogurt Spinach Artichoke Dip

Prep time: 30 minutes

Servings: 16

Ingredients

- 14 oz. can artichoke hearts, drained and chopped
- 10 oz. pack frozen spinach, thawed
- 1 1/3 cups plain Greek yogurt
- 2 garlic cloves, minced
- 2/3 cup mozzarella, shredded
- 1/3 cup Parmesan, shredded
- 6 oz. feta, crumbled

Instructions

1. Preheat the oven to 350 F and grease a casserole dish and set aside.
2. Squeeze out the liquid completely from the spinach and transfer it to a bowl.
3. Add in the rest of ingredients to it. Fold the ingredients with a spoon to mix well.
4. Transfer the mixture to the prepared baking dish. Top with more Parmesan and mozzarella.
5. Bake for 30 minutes. Broil for last 5 minutes.
6. Once cooked, serve.

Nutritional info (per serving): 83 calories; 4 g fat; 4 g total carbs; 8 g protein

Fig Smoothie With Cinnamon

Prep time: 10 minutes

Servings: 2

Ingredients

- 3 dessertspoons porridge oats
- 1 large ripe fig
- 6 ¾ oz. orange juice
- 3 rounded dessertspoons Greek yogurt
- ½ teaspoon ground cinnamon
- 3 ice cubes

Instructions

1. Wash and dry the fig and chop roughly. Reserve some for topping.
2. Add all ingredients to a blender, except for the ice cubes.
3. Add a little water to thin the smoothie and add an ice cube at the end.
4. Top with some cinnamon, a teaspoon of yogurt, and reserved fig. Finally, serve.

Nutritional info (per serving): 92 calories; 1.1 g fat; 20 g total carbs; 3 g protein

Smoked Salmon Avocado And Cucumber Bites

Prep time: 10 minutes

Servings: 12 bites

Ingredients

- 1 large avocado, peeled and pit removed
- 1 medium cucumber
- 6 oz. smoked salmon
- ½ tablespoon lime juice
- chives
- black pepper

Instructions

1. Cut the cucumber into ¼ inch thick pieces and lay flat on a plate.
2. Add the lime juice and the avocado to a bowl and mash with a fork until creamy.
3. Spread avocado on each cucumber and add a slice of salmon on top.
4. Add black pepper and chives on each bite.
5. Once cooked, serve.

Nutritional info (per serving): 46 calories; 3 g fat; 2 g total carbs; 3 g protein

Baked Root Vegetable Chips With Buttermilk Parsley Dipping Sauce

Prep time: 40 minutes

Servings: 2 cups of chips

Ingredients

- 6 tablespoons buttermilk
- 7 oz. cup 2% Greek yogurt
- 2 garlic cloves, minced
- 1 teaspoon honey
- 1 teaspoon lemon zest
- 2 tablespoons parsley, minced
- Salt

- 1 large parsnip
- 1 medium turnip
- 1 medium red beet
- 1 medium golden beet
- ½ teaspoon dried thyme
- 2 tablespoons olive oil
- 1 teaspoon garlic powder
- ½ teaspoon ground cumin
- ¼ teaspoon kosher salt

Instructions

1. Mix the first 7 ingredients in a bowl to make the buttermilk-parsley dipping sauce. Cover and refrigerate until ready.
2. Whisk the thyme, oil, ground cumin, garlic powder, and salt in a bowl. Peel all the root veggies and slice them 1/8 inch thick. Brush each side of the chip with oil and add to an oven-safe wire rack.
3. Preheat the oven to 400 F. Place baking sheets in the oven and bake for 20 minutes.
4. Once cooked, serve with sauce.

Nutritional info (per serving): 66 calories; 3 g fat; 7 g total carbs; 3 g protein

Spicy Red Lentil Dip

Prep time: 25 minutes   **Servings:** 4

Ingredients

- 2 teaspoons curry powder
- 1 cup red lentils, picked over, and rinsed
- 1 teaspoon onion powder
- ¼ teaspoon turmeric
- ½ teaspoon cumin
- ½ teaspoon Garam masala
- 1 teaspoon salt
- ¼ teaspoon black pepper
- crackers

Instructions

1. Add the lentils to the pan with water to fill it by 1 inch. Bring to boil and then reduce heat to low. Cook for 20 minutes. Drain off any excess water.
2. Mash the lentils with a fork. Add the spices and mix.
3. Once cooked, serve the dip with crackers.

Nutritional info (per serving): 228 calories; 3.8 g fat; 38 g total carbs; 12 g protein

Cucumber Hummus Sandwiches

Prep time: 5 minutes

Servings: 1

Ingredients

- 10 round slices cucumber
- 5 teaspoons hummus

Instructions

1. Add 1 teaspoon hummus on one slice of cucumber. Top with another slice and serve.

Nutritional info (per serving): 54 calories; 2.1 g fat; 7 g total carbs; 2 g protein

Blackberries Caprese Skewers

Prep time: 15 minutes

Servings: 4

Ingredients

- ½ cup cherry tomatoes
- 4 fresh basil leaves
- 4 blackberries
- ¼ cup baby mozzarella balls

Instructions

1. Put blackberries, tomatoes, mozzarella balls, and basil on skewers.
2. Once done, serve.

Nutritional info (per serving): 40 calories; 1.7 g fat; 4 g total carbs; 2 g protein

Tomato Basil Skewers

Prep time: 15 minutes

Servings: 6

Ingredients

- 16 cherry tomatoes
- 16 fresh basil leaves
- 16 small fresh mozzarella balls
- olive oil
- salt and black pepper

Instructions

1. Put mozzarella, basil, and tomatoes on skewers.
2. Add the oil and season well.
3. Once done, serve.

Nutritional info (per serving): 46 calories; 3.3 g fat; 1 g total carbs; 2.8 g protein

Fig and Ricotta Toast

Prep time: 10 minutes

Servings: 1

Ingredients

- 1 fresh fig dried, sliced
- 1 slice crusty whole-grain bread
- ¼ cup part-skim ricotta cheese
- 1 teaspoon honey
- 1 teaspoon sliced almonds, toasted
- pinch flaky sea salt

Instructions

1. Toast the bread and add the figs, ricotta cheese, and almonds on it.
2. Add honey on top, season with sea salt, and serve.

Nutritional info (per serving): 252 calories; 9.1 g fat; 32.1 g total carbs; 12.5 g protein

Date Wraps

Prep time: 10 minutes

Servings: 16 bites

Ingredients

- 16 whole pitted dates
- 16 thin slices prosciutto
- pepper

Instructions

1. Place prosciutto slice flat on a plate. Put a date into it and wrap the slice around it.
2. Repeat with the remaining, season with pepper and serve.

Nutritional info (per serving): 35 calories; 0.8 g fat; 5.6 g total carbs; 2.2 g protein

Week 1

Shopping List

Meat and Seafood

- ☐ 12 oz. ground lamb
- ☐ 2 cans (5 0z each) oil packed tuna
- ☐ 1 cup pepperoncini
- ☐ 2 lbs. cod
- ☐ 1 lb. shrimp

Vegetables and Fruits

- ☐ 2 tomatoes
- ☐ 1 artichoke heart
- ☐ Kalamata olives
- ☐ Fresh herbs such as basil, parsley, and rosemary
- ☐ 10 oz. + 10 cups grape tomatoes
- ☐ 3 cups baby spinach
- ☐ 2 onions
- ☐ 1 orange
- ☐ 1 avocado
- ☐ 10 cups arugula
- ☐ 1 cucumber
- ☐ 1 lemon
- ☐ 1/2 cup mushrooms
- ☐ 10 garlic cloves
- ☐ 4 eggplants
- ☐ 4 cups carrots
- ☐ 12 cups lacinato kale
- ☐ 1 cup shallots
- ☐ Flat-leaf parsley leaves
- ☐ 2 (8 oz. each) packages of beets
- ☐ Fresh mint
- ☐ 8 cups mixed baby greens
- ☐ 2 lemons
- ☐ 1/2 cup capers
- ☐ 4 cups fennel
- ☐ 2 cups oil cured black olives
- ☐ 2 cups pineapple chunks
- ☐ Green onions
- ☐ Peaches
- ☐ ½ cup basil leaves

Eggs and Dairy (dairy free)

- ☐ 32 eggs
- ☐ Milk
- ☐ 1–2 slices Muenster cheese
- ☐ 1 cup + 15 oz. feta cheese
- ☐ 1 cup whole milk ricotta
- ☐ 4 (1 oz.) slices + 1 ½ cups mozzarella cheese
- ☐ 2 tablespoons butter
- ☐ 3 tablespoons cream cheese
- ☐ 1/2 cup sour cream, reduced-fat
- ☐ 3 ½ cups heavy whipping cream
- ☐ 3 cups mascarpone cheese
- ☐ Butter
- ☐ 5 oz. Greek yogurt
- ☐ 32 oz. cream cheese
- ☐ 2 cups double cream
- ☐ 2 cups plain Greek yogurt
- ☐ 1 ½ cups mozzarella
- ☐ 2/3 cup parmesan

Pasta, Nuts, and Grains

- ☐ 1 whole grain seeded ciabatta roll
- ☐ 2 cups quinoa
- ☐ 1 1/2 cups almonds
- ☐ Hearty whole grain toast, English muffin, or bagel
- ☐ 2 English muffin
- ☐ 4 cups bulgur
- ☐ 1¼ cups couscous
- ☐ 1 cup basmati rice
- ☐ 2 7 oz. pack Italian Lady fingers
- ☐ 9 oz. digestive biscuits

Canned and Frozen

- ☐ 2 (15 oz. each) cans chickpeas
- ☐ 20 oz. pack frozen spinach
- ☐ 28 oz. can artichoke hearts
- ☐ 2 cans (14.5 oz. each) diced tomato

Sauces and Liquids

- ☐ 1 tablespoon Romesco sauce
- ☐ Pesto
- ☐ Extra-virgin olive oil
- ☐ Sunflower oil
- ☐ Almond extract
- ☐ Honey
- ☐ Distilled white vinegar
- ☐ 1¼ cups marinara sauce, store-bought or homemade
- ☐ Canola oil
- ☐ Tahini
- ☐ 1/2 cup pineapple juice
- ☐ 1 tablespoon lime juice
- ☐ 1 tablespoon maple syrup
- ☐ 1 cup cold espresso
- ☐ 1 teaspoon vanilla essence
- ☐ 1 cup any jam

Spices and Powders

- ☐ Salt
- ☐ Pepper
- ☐ Sea salt
- ☐ Ground turmeric
- ☐ Ground cumin
- ☐ 1 oz. almond flour
- ☐ 1 teaspoon orange zest
- ☐ Garlic powder
- ☐ 1/4 teaspoon red pepper, crushed
- ☐ Onion powder
- ☐ Curry powder
- ☐ 2 1/4 teaspoon Caribbean jerk seasoning
- ☐ 1 cup sugar
- ☐ 1 oz. unsweetened cocoa
- ☐ 4 oz. icing sugar

Day 1

Breakfast
Mediterranean Omelette

Lunch
Eggplant Pizza

Dinner
Couscous with Tuna and Pepperoncini

Dessert
Tiramisu

Day 2

Breakfast
Egg White Breakfast Sandwich

Lunch
Eggplant Pizza

Dinner
Couscous with Tuna and Pepperoncini

Dessert
Tiramisu

Day 3

Breakfast
Egg Muffins with Veggies and Feta

Lunch
Kale Chickpeas Grain Bowl

Dinner
Mediterranean Cod

Snack
Greek Yogurt Spinach Artichoke Dip

Day 4

Breakfast
Honey Almond Ricotta Spread with Fruits

Lunch
Kale Chickpeas Grain Bowl

Dinner
Mediterranean Cod

Snack
Greek Yogurt Spinach Artichoke Dip

Day 5

Breakfast
Poached Eggs Caprese

Lunch
Lamb and Beet Meatballs

Dinner
Shrimp with Pineapple Rice

Dessert
Greek Cheesecake with Yogurt

Day 6

Breakfast
Mediterranean Breakfast Salad

Lunch
Lamb and Beet Meatballs

Dinner
Shrimp with Pineapple Rice

Dessert
Greek Cheesecake with Yogurt

Day 7

Breakfast
Eggs Florentine

Lunch
Eggplant Pizza

Dinner
Couscous with Tuna and Pepperoncini

Dessert
Greek Yogurt Spinach Artichoke Dip

Week 2

Shopping List

Meat and Seafood

- [ ] 2 smoked spinach and feta chicken sausages
- [ ] 2 lbs. raw medium shrimp
- [ ] 5 lbs. boneless skinless chicken breasts
- [ ] 8 (6 oz.) skinless salmon fillets

Vegetables and Fruits

- [ ] 4 dates
- [ ] 5 dried apricots, finely chopped
- [ ] ½ cup fresh shiitake mushrooms
- [ ] 1 cup fresh baby spinach
- [ ] 6 fresh sage leaves
- [ ] 1 cucumber
- [ ] 4 bell peppers
- [ ] ½ cup tomatoes
- [ ] ½ cup green onions
- [ ] 3 lbs. asparagus, trimmed
- [ ] 3 leeks
- [ ] 8 oz. Baby Bella mushrooms
- [ ] 7 avocados
- [ ] 3 zucchini
- [ ] 3 cups Brussels sprouts
- [ ] 3 cups kale leaves
- [ ] 7 garlic cloves
- [ ] Fresh dill
- [ ] 8 oz. haricots verts (French green beans)
- [ ] 2 cups Japanese eggplant
- [ ] Fresh thyme
- [ ] 8 cups cherry tomatoes
- [ ] 1/2 cup mint or basil leaves
- [ ] 3 1/2 cups cooked chickpeas
- [ ] 1/2 cup parsley leaves
- [ ] 1/4 cup green olives
- [ ] 1 jalapeno
- [ ] 1/3 cup Kalamata olives
- [ ] 3–5 green onions
- [ ] 1/2 teaspoon Aleppo pepper

- [ ] 2 lemons
- [ ] 1 lime
- [ ] Fresh cilantro
- [ ] 1 tablespoon tarragon
- [ ] 2 ½ cups sugar snap peas
- [ ] 2/3 cup shallots
- [ ] 8 oranges
- [ ] 2 ripe figs
- [ ] 1 banana

Eggs and Dairy (dairy free)

- [ ] 2 cups milk
- [ ] 29 eggs
- [ ] Butter
- [ ] 1 ½ cups sharp cheddar cheese
- [ ] ½ cup skim milk
- [ ] ¼ cup feta
- [ ] 1 cup Parmesan cheese
- [ ] 1 cup goat cheese
- [ ] ¾ cup almond milk or any non-dairy milk of choice
- [ ] 1/4 cup heavy cream
- [ ] 1 ½ tablespoons canola mayonnaise
- [ ] 5 cups strained Greek yogurt
- [ ] 7 oz. dark couverture chocolate

Pasta, Nuts, and Grains

- [ ] 1/4 cup raw almonds
- [ ] 2 1/2 cups quinoa
- [ ] 1 cup rolled oats
- [ ] 1 ½ tablespoons chia seeds
- [ ] 8 oz. spaghetti, whole-grain
- [ ] 8 oz. casarecce, fusilli, or penne pasta, uncooked
- [ ] 6 oz. burrata
- [ ] ½ cup whole-wheat panko
- [ ] 1 cup + 7 oz. walnuts
- [ ] 3 dessert spoons of porridge oats
- [ ] 4 tostadas

Canned and Frozen

- ☐ 2 cups baby sweet peas, frozen
- ☐ 1/2 cup sun-dried tomatoes
- ☐ 11 oz. Pillsbury thin pizza crust, refrigerated

Sauces and Liquids

- ☐ Vanilla extract
- ☐ Honey
- ☐ ½ cup red pepper hummus
- ☐ Olive oil
- ☐ ½ cup strong coffee
- ☐ ½ cup hummus
- ☐ Dijon mustard
- ☐ White wine vinegar
- ☐ 1/4 cup dry white wine
- ☐ Red wine vinegar
- ☐ 6 oz. tahini
- ☐ 2 oz. cognac
- ☐ 6 ¾ oz. orange juice

Spices and Powders

- ☐ Ground cinnamon
- ☐ Sea salt
- ☐ Black pepper
- ☐ Salt
- ☐ Garlic powder
- ☐ Oregano
- ☐ Red-pepper flakes
- ☐ 2 tablespoons cocoa powder
- ☐ Ground sumac
- ☐ 1/4 cup flour
- ☐ Ground cumin
- ☐ Cinnamon powder
- ☐ 5 ½ oz. all-purpose flour
- ☐ Baking powder
- ☐ 5 oz. icing sugar

Day 1

Breakfast
Breakfast Quinoa

Lunch
Shrimp and Leek Spaghetti

Dinner
Lemon Chicken with Asparagus

Dessert
Greek Yogurt and Honey Walnuts

Day 2

Breakfast
Mediterranean Breakfast Buns

Lunch
Shrimp and Leek Spaghetti

Dinner
Lemon Chicken with Asparagus

Dessert
Greek Yogurt and Honey Walnuts

Day 3

Breakfast
Breakfast Tostadas

Lunch
Pasta Salad with Tomatoes and
Eggplant

Dinner
Cilantro Lime Chicken

Snack
Fig Smoothie With Cinnamon

Day 4

Breakfast
Mediterranean Frittata

Lunch
Pasta Salad with Tomatoes and
Eggplant

Dinner
Cilantro Lime Chicken

Snack
Fig Smoothie With Cinnamon

Day 5

Breakfast
Baked Eggs and Zoodles

Lunch
Balela Salad

Dinner
Panko Salmon With Snap Peas

Dessert
Chocolate Brownies

Day 6

Breakfast
Banana Mocha Overnight Oats

Lunch
Balela Salad

Dinner
Panko Salmon With Snap Peas

Dessert
Chocolate Brownies

Day 7

Breakfast
Hummus and Veggies Bowl

Lunch
Pasta Salad with Tomatoes and Eggplant

Dinner
Lemon Chicken with Asparagus

Dessert
Greek Yogurt and Honey Walnuts

Week 3

Shopping List

Meat and Seafood

- [ ] 1 lb. chicken breast cutlets
- [ ] 6 oz. smoked salmon

Vegetables and Fruits

- [ ] 2 avocados
- [ ] 3 cups spinach
- [ ] 1 banana
- [ ] 1 apple
- [ ] 8 tomatoes
- [ ] Fresh herbs
- [ ] 3 English cucumbers
- [ ] 2 cups fresh mint leaves
- [ ] 3 cups fresh parsley leaves
- [ ] 5 radishes
- [ ] 5 green onions
- [ ] 5 Roma tomatoes
- [ ] 1 heart Romaine lettuce
- [ ] 5 limes
- [ ] 1 red onion
- [ ] 2 1/2 celery stalks
- [ ] 4–5 whole radishes
- [ ] 1/2 cup Kalamata olives
- [ ] 3 green onions
- [ ] 1 onion
- [ ] 2 cups baby spinach
- [ ] 4 garlic cloves
- [ ] 1 carrot
- [ ] 1 celery rib
- [ ] 8 oz. haricots verts
- [ ] 2 cups Japanese eggplant
- [ ] 33.25 oz. cherry tomatoes
- [ ] 5 oz. baby spinach
- [ ] ½ cup jarred roasted red peppers
- [ ] 1 plum tomato, chopped
- [ ] 4 cups packed arugula
- [ ] 2 cups cherry tomatoes
- [ ] 4 peaches
- [ ] 4 nectarines
- [ ] ½ mango
- [ ] 1 ¼ lbs. sweet cherries
- [ ] 1 lime

Eggs and Dairy (dairy free)

- [ ] 11 eggs
- [ ] 4 cups milk
- [ ] Yogurt
- [ ] Parmesan cheese
- [ ] 1 ½ oz. Manchego cheese
- [ ] 1 cup salted butter
- [ ] Butter

Pasta, Nuts, and Grains

- [ ] ½ cup chia seeds
- [ ] 1/2 cup rolled oats
- [ ] 1 cup steel-cut oats
- [ ] 2 pita bread loaves
- [ ] Pita chips/pita pockets
- [ ] 8 oz. casarecce pasta
- [ ] 6 oz. burrata
- [ ] 16 oz. whole-wheat potato gnocchi
- [ ] ¼ cup smoked almonds
- [ ] 1 baguette slice
- [ ] 2/3 cup bulgur
- [ ] 8 speculoos cookies

Canned and Frozen

- [ ] 1 cup berries of choice, frozen
- [ ] 3 cans (5 oz. each) tuna
- [ ] 3 cans (15 oz. each) white beans

Sauces and Liquids

- [ ] Honey
- [ ] 2 cups coconut water
- [ ] Maple syrup
- [ ] Olive oil
- [ ] 2 1/2 teaspoons Dijon mustard
- [ ] 6 cups vegetable broth
- [ ] ¼ cup dry white wine

- ☐ 2 teaspoons white wine vinegar
- ☐ 2 tablespoons sherry vinegar
- ☐ 2 tablespoons rice vinegar
- ☐ Vanilla extract
- ☐ Almond extract

Spices and Powders

- ☐ Salt
- ☐ Cinnamon
- ☐ Black pepper
- ☐ Sumac
- ☐ Ground allspice
- ☐ Dried thyme
- ☐ Oregano
- ☐ Paprika
- ☐ Red pepper, crushed
- ☐ ¼ cup brown sugar
- ☐ 1 ½ cups flour
- ☐ ½ cup + 3 tablespoons sugar

Day 1

Breakfast
Avocado and Apple Smoothie

Lunch
Fattoush Salad

Dinner
Warm Pasta Salad with Tomatoes And Eggplant

Dessert
Peach Nectarine Mango Crumble

Day 2

Breakfast
Berry Chia Overnight Oats

Lunch
Fattoush Salad

Dinner
Warm Pasta Salad with Tomatoes And Eggplant

Dessert
Peach Nectarine Mango Crumble

Day 3

Breakfast
Avocado and Apple Smoothie

Lunch
Tuna Salad with Dijon Mustard Vinaigrette

Dinner
Gnocchi with Spinach And Pepper Sauce

Snack
Smoked Salmon, Avocado and Cucumber Bites

Day 4

Breakfast
Berry Chia Overnight Oats

Lunch
Tuna Salad with Dijon Mustard Vinaigrette

Dinner
Gnocchi with Spinach and Pepper Sauce

Snack
Smoked Salmon, Avocado and Cucumber Bites

Day 5

Breakfast
Savory Steel Cut Oatmeal

Lunch
White Bean Soup

Dinner
Chicken and Bulgur Salad With Peaches

Dessert
Cherry Clafoutis

Day 6

Breakfast
Eggs Baked in Tomatoes

Lunch
White Bean Soup

Dinner
Chicken and Bulgur Salad With Peaches

Dessert
Cherry Clafoutis

Day 7

Breakfast
Savory Steel Cut Oatmeal

Lunch
Fattoush Salad

Dinner
Warm Pasta Salad with Tomatoes And Eggplant

Dessert
Cherry Clafoutis

Shopping List

Meat and Seafood

- [ ] 1 link chicken andouille sausage
- [ ] 2 lbs. 93% lean ground turkey
- [ ] 16 (4 oz.) lamb rib chops
- [ ] 8 (6 oz.) yellow fin tuna steaks

Vegetables and Fruits

- [ ] 9 tomatoes
- [ ] 1 cup tomatoes, cherry or grape tomatoes
- [ ] 1 artichoke heart
- [ ] 2 cups Kalamata olives
- [ ] 10 oz. grape tomatoes, halved
- [ ] 2 cups baby spinach
- [ ] Fresh oregano
- [ ] 6 onions
- [ ] 1 orange
- [ ] 1/3 cup celery
- [ ] 2 celery stalks
- [ ] 1/3 cup + 2 carrots
- [ ] 10 garlic cloves
- [ ] 1 cup fresh baby spinach
- [ ] 5 zucchini
- [ ] 3 bell peppers
- [ ] 3 ½ oz. capers
- [ ] 2 cups arugula
- [ ] ½ cup cucumber, sliced
- [ ] 1 tablespoon orange juice
- [ ] 1 orange
- [ ] ¼ cup green onions
- [ ] Parsley
- [ ] 1 lemon
- [ ] 1 blood orange
- [ ] 3 lemons
- [ ] 1 parsnip
- [ ] 1 turnip
- [ ] 1 red beet
- [ ] 1 golden beet
- [ ] Fresh herbs such as basil, parsley and rosemary
- [ ] Peaches

Eggs and Dairy (dairy free)

- [ ] Feta cheese, 1 block
- [ ] 20 eggs
- [ ] 1 tablespoon milk or cream
- [ ] 1–2 slices Muenster cheese
- [ ] 1 cup whole milk ricotta
- [ ] 1/3 cup whole-wheat Greek yogurt
- [ ] ½ cup whole-milk plain yogurt
- [ ] 7 oz. unsalted butter
- [ ] 6 tablespoons buttermilk
- [ ] 7 oz. cup 2% Greek yogurt

Pasta, Nuts, and Grains

- [ ] 1 whole grain seeded ciabatta roll
- [ ] 1 cup quinoa
- [ ] 1/2 cup almonds
- [ ] Hearty whole grain toast, English muffin or bagel
- [ ] ½ cup small shell pasta
- [ ] ½ cup medium-grind oatmeal
- [ ] 1 cup red lentils
- [ ] ¾ cup polenta
- [ ] 4 whole-wheat hamburger buns

Canned and Frozen

- [ ] 1/2 cup roasted tomatoes
- [ ] 15 oz. can cannellini beans
- [ ] 28 oz. can crushed tomatoes

Sauces and Liquids

- [ ] 1 tablespoon Romesco sauce
- [ ] 1 tablespoon pesto
- [ ] Extra-virgin olive oil
- [ ] Sunflower oil
- [ ] Almond extract
- [ ] Honey
- [ ] 3 cups low sodium chicken broth

- 32 ounce vegetable broth
- 8 cups chickens stock
- 5 oz. concentrated tomato puree
- ¼ cup canola mayonnaise
- 3 tablespoons balsamic vinegar
- Vanilla extract

Spices and Powders

- Salt
- Pepper
- Dried oregano
- Ground cumin
- Ground coriander
- 1 ¼ cup all-purpose flour
- Baking powder
- Baking soda
- 1 2/3 cups + 2 tablespoons granulated sugar
- Fine sea salt
- 2 cups almond flour
- ½ cup powdered sugar
- Dried thyme
- Garlic powder

Day 1

Breakfast
Mediterranean Omelette

Lunch
Lentil Soup

Dinner
Greek Turkey Burgers

Dessert
Blood Orange Olive Oil Cake

Day 2

Breakfast
Egg White Breakfast Sandwich

Lunch
Lentil Soup

Dinner
Orange-Balsamic Lamb Chops

Dessert
Blood Orange Olive Oil Cake

Day 3

Breakfast
Mediterranean Omelette

Lunch
Vegetable Soup

Dinner
Greek Turkey Burgers

Snack
Baked Root Vegetable Chips With
Buttermilk-Parsley Dipping Sauce

Day 4

Breakfast
Egg White Breakfast Sandwich

Lunch
Vegetable Soup

Dinner
Orange-Balsamic Lamb Chops

Snack
Baked Root Vegetable Chips With
Buttermilk-Parsley Dipping Sauce

Day 5

Breakfast
Egg Muffins with Veggies and Feta

Lunch
Mediterranean Chicken Soup

Dinner
Seared Mediterranean Tuna Steaks

Dessert
Gluten-Free Lemon Cake

Day 6

Breakfast
Honey Almond Ricotta Spread with
Fruits

Lunch
Mediterranean Chicken Soup

Dinner
Seared Mediterranean Tuna Steaks

Dessert
Gluten-Free Lemon Cake

Day 7

Breakfast
Egg Muffins with Veggies and Feta

Lunch
Mediterranean Chicken Soup

Dinner
Orange-Balsamic Lamb Chops

Dessert
Gluten-Free Lemon Cake

Made in the USA
Coppell, TX
11 August 2020